MY FAVORITE HORROR MOVIE
3
SCREAM WARRIORS

MY FAVORITE HORROR MOVIE 3
SCREAM WARRIORS

EDITED & CURATED BY

CHRISTIAN ACKERMAN,
FELISSA ROSE &
CHUCK FOSTER

BLACK VORTEX CINEMA

Published by
Black Vortex Cinema
1800 N. La Brea
Los Angeles, CA 90046

INTERIOR LAYOUT/COVER PHOTO: CHRISTIAN ACKERMAN
COVER DESIGN: JOSH MCKEVITT
JOSHMCKEVITT.COM

ADDITIONAL EDITING: JENNIFER FOSTER

JOIN US!

WEB:
BLACKVORTEXCINEMA.COM

FACEBOOK/INSTAGRAM:
@MYFAVORITEHORRORMOVIE

TWITTER:
@MYFAVEHORROR

ISBN: 978-1-7322702-3-7

"What scares me is what scares you.
We're all afraid of the same things.
That's why horror is such a powerful genre.
All you have to do is ask yourself what
frightens you and you'll know what frightens me."

-John Carpenter

BODY PARTS

INTRODUCTION

BY

CHRISTIAN ACKERMAN

Welcome to *My Favorite Horror Movie 3: Scream Warriors*, because trilogies must always come in threes! "Why *Scream Warriors*?" you may ask. Besides my favorite horror movie being *A Nightmare on Elm Street 3: Dream Warriors*, as horror fans like you, we as filmmakers and bookmakers live and die to experience terror in our art. We can't get enough screams.

Buried deep within these pages is a massive amount of blood, sweat, and tears from legends and luminaries I massively admire. Boils and ghouls who have dedicated their lives to disturbing our sleep patterns. I want to thank each and every one of them for spilling their guts all over these chapters.

No book of this scale is made alone, so I wish to acknowledge the team: our cover design wizard Josh McKevitt and co-editors and curators, Felissa Rose and Chuck Foster. Making these books with them has been an absolute pleasure.

Lastly, I want to thank all of you for picking up this tome. I hope it inspires you like the horror books I've picked up in my life when I felt that I was the only horror fan I knew.

Scream on, Scream Warriors!

THE POWER OF HORROR COMPELS YOU!

PET SEMATARY (1989)
BY
DAN CRAWLEY

Special Effects & Makeup Artist
Captain Marvel, Deadpool, Thor, Apocalypto
The Curious Case of Benjamin Button
Facebook: @Dan.Crawley.56 Instagram: @DanMakesStuff

For me, movies can be like a time machine. Certain films just have an incredible and indescribable way of instantly transporting me back to that moment in my life when I first saw them. Out of the hundreds of movies we see in our lives, most of them are probably in and immediately right back out of our minds. If I asked you for specifics, you probably couldn't recall the plot, characters, or even that you saw half of them in the first place. Every once in a while though, there's that special one that sticks with you.

This may seem like a shock (coming from a guy with tattooed sleeves of Basil Gogos' paintings of old *Famous Monsters of Filmland* covers depicting the classic Universal Monsters), but I'm actually not really a big horror movie fan. I honestly just

love some of the imagery, storytelling, and thought-provok-
ing ideas or social commentaries illustrated via their morbid
or phantasmic allegory. Watching the violent and/or shocking
images play out often is just a bit much for me to handle. That's
not to say I don't have profound moments of identification and
passion for the genre, which have definitely shaped both my life
and my taste in aesthetics.

At a sleepover with friends when I was around age 12, I'll
never forget watching my first horror, *Friday the 13th Part VI:
Jason Lives*. I was filled with dread and apprehension, but also
curious excitement. It wasn't so much about what I was going
to see (although that was part of it), but more about the thrash-
ing I'd take from my buddies if I even flinched for a second or
showed any sign of fear.

By my late teens, I was gobbling up every piece of B-movie
horror garbage I could get my hands on. Ok, maybe "garbage"
isn't fair, but I wasn't looking for high art at that point. I was
seduced by novelty, unfamiliarity, and the shocking nature of it
all. As with any adolescent, a healthy amount of the attraction
was wanting to freak out my parents, friends, and everybody
at school in my small, conservative hometown. At that point,
it was the heavy-hitters: Jason, Freddy, Leatherface, Pinhead,
and Chucky, with a healthy smattering of Troma VHS releases.
These were the places I was most likely to catch plenty of gore
and maybe a boob or two (although that likely was right before
the poor girl was murdered by said heavy, so I'm not really sure
if that was healthy).

Eventually, I made my way to and fell in love with the good
stuff: the Universal monster movies from the 1930s through
the late '40s, German expressionism and art deco, classics from
Hitchcock, and of course *The Exorcist* (right around this time
it came back to theaters as the director's cut with the infamous
"spider walk" scene). Now I was really starting to discover and
understand this genre.

While all of these movies were unique in their own way
and somewhat formative for me, they've already been writ-

ten about endlessly. They've been analyzed by scholars, used in collegiate courses, deconstructed and reinterpreted a thousand times. We've all read about them, watched them, quoted them, and they all feel like old friends anytime we revisit them. For this essay though, I wanted to dig a little deeper and think about one of the less obvious movies that has the thrilling ability to instantly zap me back to a special place in time.

Then it came to me...much like a number of its protagonists would to their loved ones. *Pet Sematary*.

Where does this movie transport me to? It was one of the happiest times in my life, with one of my best friends, where I worked in an amazing crew that I'm still friends with to this day - two of whom are involved in the publishing of this book. The year was 2005, and I had been working in the film industry for only about five years at the time as a makeup effects artist. How'd I end up doing that? It probably had something to do with how some of the aforementioned films influenced me and a certain serendipitous moment at that adolescent sleepover, but I digress.

In the fall of 2005, with Halloween (my favorite holiday), fast approaching, I was contracted to do all of the makeup effects on a low-budget horror film that was the passion project of a number of really talented people. Honestly, that part was just a bonus and didn't matter as much to me as that at point in my career where I would take every project I could get my hands on. It was such an exciting time and felt like I was on the cusp of something big. I was ready to make my mark on the world one splash of blood at a time. Long story short? It was a zombie film. So what did my best friend and I do? We watched a ton of zombie movies to research and get inspired of course!

My right-hand man/best friend was Chris Hampton, and this guy had an encyclopedic knowledge of horror films, especially zombie films. He lived and breathed Romero and was determined to follow in his footsteps. As we spent our days merrily chipping away at the mountain of makeup effects in the back shed of a local business, he introduced me to tens of horror classics daily. That DVD player burned through discs as we built severed heads, arms, and a myriad of zombie teeth and prosthetics. Honestly, most of the movies we watched weren't that great. I don't even remember half of them, but one really did stand out for me. It stands out to this day, becoming one of my favorite movies of all time - *Pet Sematary*. Is it a zombie movie? Well, not really...but people and animals do come back from the dead, so that kind of counts? It doesn't really matter.

The makeup effects by legendary David Anderson blew my mind. Sure, some are hokey and even a bit theatrical, but some are downright terrifying. I must've studied the Pascow makeup every day that we worked in the shop. I can distinctly remember pausing the film repeatedly and studying all of the fine line work of the veins and capillaries. Although I was an artist of my time and married to the use of airbrush for pretty much everything, this makeup was beautifully hand painted by brush like a tapestry by one of the masters. In every lighting scenario, it just read so beautifully. The character himself is one you can empathize with. A "good" dead guy in a sea of evil, wicked, violent dead things. Or is he even there at all? Maybe he's just a ghost in Louis Creed's machine.

That's the beauty of this movie. It blurs the line between what's real and what's not. We are asked to question what is actually happening, and what is the unraveling of the damaged and desperate mind of a father who makes progressively horrible choices. It asks us to reflect and examine ourselves should we be put into the same set of circumstances. The best part comes at the end, when you still don't get any answers or closure. It leaves you hanging in the midst of a bleak and terrible outcome with no hope for the future. It's a rare and bold choice that dares not to neatly wrap the resolution in a bow.

For all of its strengths, this movie also has the tendency to tonally sway all over the road. One minute it's a cheesy, over-acted, parody-like exchange in a painfully bland setting. The next minute it, zags into moments of dealing with genuine emotions like fear, sadness, longing, and intensity. It caps off with some really impactful moments of tension and dread peppered in. To this day, the scene where Jud recounts the story of Timmy Baterman's story is still as malevolent and terrifying for me as the first time I watched it. This movie is a recipe of the most random ingredients, but somehow, it all comes together to work for me now as it did then.

Is it a great film? Not really. Does it have some great moments? That's subjective I suppose, but I'd argue that it does - and maybe that's really what it's all about. Who knows why the things that resonate with us make their presence known at the moment that they do. Maybe it was just the concurrence of events and phenomenon of that time. Should our paths have crossed otherwise it may have continued to be forgotten or blurred in my subconscious. For me though, it still conjures a time when my life was simpler, and I got to have some of the most fun I've ever had with one of my best buddies and one of the best groups of people. It came at the right time for me. Nearly 15 years later, I still watch it every fall and let it be one of those special "time machine movies."

PSYCHO (1960)
BY
TOM HOLLAND

Writer/Director
Fright Night, Child's Play, Psycho II
TerrorTime.com TerrorTime.shop
Facebook: @THTerrorTime

I pulled the collar of my hound's tooth coat up around my ears to take a bite out of the freezing winter wind. It was March '61. I had taken the train into the city for a Saturday acting class in the Village. The train was late, so I missed the start of class. Now, I was kicking around, trying to decide the rest of my day. If I went home, I'd spend the afternoon working in my parents' women's wear shop, and let's face it, that was what I was trying to avoid by taking acting classes in the city. If I had gone into class late, I most certainly would have gotten a lecture on wasting people's time. I was 16. What 16-year-old wants a lecture?

I weighed my options and took off toward the uptown subway. The idea was a simple one: I could kill a couple of hours at the movies, make like I went to class, and waste just enough time to not have to restock the shelves at my folk's store. I rode the subway to Times Square and trudged along the street, staring up at the stream of marquees.

It was that miserable season in the city where everything was cold, grey, and perpetually wet; the time of year that always made Simon and Garfunkel sing about going home. I pulled a Chesterfield out of a pack I'd taken from the icebox this morning. My mother kept a carton there to keep them fresh and didn't seem to notice, or at least she never mentioned, the occasional pack I nicked from her stash. I paused to light it in front of a theater showing George Pal's adaptation of H.G. Well's *The Time Machine*.

This was a time in my life when science fiction and fantasy had a pretty firm grip on my soul. Heinlein, Asimov, Clarke, Howard, Wells…pretty much anything I could get my hands on. I traded books with a small group of other outcasts who had similar interests, and it was this group of friends that would lead to my eventual discovery of EC and Atlas comics, and the bizarre tales of horror that would be a huge influence on my later life. But that's a longer story for another time…

The Time Machine it was…or not. I approached the box office and peered inside. Empty. I tapped on the glass and waited. Nothing. No one came. While I stood there, a few people lined up behind me. I looked back at them and shrugged. As I walked away, I glanced over my shoulder to watch them one at a time duplicate my earlier actions: the peering, the tapping, and the shrugging. No success. I wandered on. Maybe another theater would be showing it further down.

As I walked down the street, I saw a short line in front of a little "second run" theater. Alfred Hitchcock's *Psycho* was on the marquee above. The weathered poster in the "Now Showing" box was a warning from Hitchcock himself that you must see this movie from the beginning. Well, I was here now and the movie was about to start, so I bought my ticket and took my chances.

I'd heard a little about Psycho before it came out, but it never landed in the theater in my hometown, and it was only since I started taking acting classes that I found myself travelling into the city alone. My only real knowledge about it was from one or two of my fellow sci-fi outcasts who'd seen it and come away from it absolutely terrified and shaken. But how bad could it be? After all, it's only a movie...

It starts with the terrifying screeching strings. Saul Bass' out-of-the-darkness slashing opening title credits create a frenetic vision to match the music. From the beginning, you are unsettled. But then Phoenix...and Janet Leigh....and the small matter of the theft of $40,000...and you settle into what appears to be a rather typical Hitchcock thriller, except for the nagging, ominous Bernard Hermann score that doesn't ever quite let you sit back in your seat. By the time Leigh arrives at the Bates Motel, there is a kind of relief, as you have spent most of the last 20 minutes expecting something horrible; some reversal of fortune for Leigh, an arrest, or maybe the theft or loss of the money.

Norman Bates was played to perfection by Tony Perkins. Sympathy. That was the feeling he most invoked in me. I watched him shackled to that roadside motel, forever under the thumb of his crazy, domineering mother. My empathizing with his plight might have been a reaction to the dread I felt at my own family wanting me to sell ladies wear in upstate New York for the rest of my life. His characterization, and how I felt sorry for him, stuck with me hard, and would be the basis for how I envisioned and detailed Norman when I wrote *Psycho II*.

Janet Leigh gets killed in the shower. It came out of nowhere. Like heat lightning. I remember watching it unfold from between my fingers. And then the camera just lingered so you couldn't look away. It forced you to watch to the very last moments of this young woman's life. You can talk about the amazing cinematography or the 70-something cuts in editing, but to me, it's always been the choice of lingering on her eye to show the light running out that always haunted me.

And now some more sympathy for Norman. Not only is he stuck running this crummy motel, but he now has to clean up everything after his mother has gone crazy and killed one of the guests. The rest of the film works because of the scene immediately following the shower kill, when Norman finds Janet Leigh's body. His visible revulsion makes everything that happens until the climax of the film seem utterly reasonable.

Not just with *Psycho*, but Hitchcock as a director had a great deal of influence on my career. I may not have gone on to direct if I hadn't risked career suicide by writing the sequel to his masterpiece. The success of *Psycho II* opened up a lot of doors for me, leading into the chance to direct *Fright Night*.

Also, if you're a fan of a certain serial killing doll, you might notice that his first kill is a homage to Arbogast getting killed on the stairs. (Smile).

FRANKENSTEIN'S ARMY

BY

HEIDI HONEYCUTT

Film Festival Director of Programming
Journalist, Author, Film Programmer
Etheria Film Festival, Fangoria Magazine,
Cat Ranch: How a Cat Ranch Saved My Life
Twitter/Instagram: @EtheriaFN Facebook: @HoneycuttHeidi

"A man of vision is always misunderstood," says Dr. Frankenstein as he wheels the body of a dazed Soviet soldier into his surgery where he will perform the ultimate act of peace: removing one half of his brain and replacing it with half of the brain of a Nazi. According to the doctor, this is the only way to unite the ideologies of both the communist and Nazi superpowers and therefore end the horrors of World War II. *Frankenstein's Army*, like its mad scientist Dr. Frankenstein, is visionary, and is largely misunderstood by mainstream critics.

While this century has had some fantastic horror in theaters such as 2013's *The Purge, The Conjuring, Contracted, We Are What We Are, Stoker,* and innovative WWII horror such as *Dead Snow* (2009), *Outpost* (2008), *Deathwatch* (2002), and *Iron Sky* (2012) had made the underground horror world very happy, it was also the time of such big-budget Hollywood shitpiles like *Hansel and Gretel: Witch Hunters* (2013), *Dracula Untold* (2014), *Dracula Reborn* (2015), *I, Frankenstein* (2014), *World War Z* (2013), *Van Helsing* (2004), *Victor Frankenstein* (2015), *Frankenstein* (2015), and travesties such as *Underworld: Blood Wars* (2016), *The Frankenstein Theory* (2013), *The Frankenstein Syndrome* (2010), *Frankenstein Vs. The Mummy* (2015), and those awful *Snow White and the Huntsman* films. There was even an *Army of Frankensteins* (2014), an entirely separate, independent film about Frankenstein's monster traveling to the United States Civil War. That one's actually not bad. However, when it came to mainstream horror in 2013, classic characters such as *Frankenstein* and *Dracula* (and God forbid we mention *The Wolf Man* remake) were churned out in fewer thoughtful films and into more badly animated computer cartoons that removed any and all gothic sensibility and poetic meaning. This is why, when *Frankenstein's Army* arrived in theaters in 2013 with promotional posters that looked an awful lot like those shitty CGI films, many filmgoers, and even horror fans, were not enthusiastic. Unceremoniously released in theaters in the United States on July 26th, 2013 by MPI Media Group and on DVD on September 10th, 2013 by MPI and Dark Sky, there's no box office information about the film other than the DVD made $63,000 according to questionable internet sources. Director/creator/madman Richard Raaphorst was interviewed by a number of film and entertainment news outlets prior to the film's release, and his intention to make an insane, crazy, gore-filled horror film should not have come as a surprise to anyone watching it. *Frankenstein's Army* exists on the fringe between Hollywood and independent European cinema; there's a place in film festivals where films like this one are extremely valued and appreciated, and there are not many spaces in the mainstream Hollywood world of Marvel superheroes and sequels for truly edgy and un-Hollywood endings.

Raaphorst is Dutch and not entirely unknown in the independent, underground horror, and film festival worlds. His unproduced horror comedy Worst Case Scenario released several trailers that made the rounds online in 2006 showcasing a filmmaking style extremely similar to what he would use for Frankenstein's Army. The film was to be narrated by Brian Yuzna and it too involved a storyline about Nazis as well as clips of actual war stock footage set to music. The project was shut down in 2009 after failing to get a budget, and not long after, in 2011, Raaphorst began work on Frankenstein's Army. Raaphorst is first and foremost an artist and film art designer; he worked in the art departments on horror films Dagon (2001) and Beyond Reanimator (2003); and created their title designs. He also created the title designs for Jovanka Vuckovic's first short film The Captured Bird (2012). His artwork, including the art designs for Frankenstein's Army, can be seen online. This intense artistry may be too much for some viewers to bear.

Frankenstein's Army stands out above the other Frankenstein-related films in theaters in 2013 mainly because Raaphorst created all of his monsters (oh and there are many) using only practical makeup and costume effects. In Matt Soller Seitz's contemporary review of the film for RogerEbert.com, he acknowledged how Frankenstein's Army differentiated itself from the CGI atrocities horror fans had been forced to endure recently: "I'd rather watch model-shop ingenuity than another $200 million CGI slugfest between superheroes or robots. Even the worst analog monsters betray a human touch." Variety's reviewers, in an unusual display of insight, wrote that the film "should put first-time director Richard Raaphorst on Hollywood's radar."

Despite this, most mainstream critics didn't like the film. It was called an "uninspired disappointment" among other things. The very questions it raises and the confusion it causes seem to be the source of unease for many. "Does the director covertly align with Frankenstein's misanthropic view of humanity?" asked Slant magazine. I mean, probably, maybe? In an original interview for this essay, director Richard Raaphorst explains that the impetus for this moral quandary was a question about humanity (or lack thereof) in war. "How can a human being slip into darkness and become a monster himself. In a war, no one is innocent. Heroes are villains too."

"He's not a doctor, he's a madman" says a shocked Soviet soldier as he sees the many horrors created by Viktor Frankenstein. But who is insane, really? Maybe Richard Raaphorst, the director himself, is insane? Or the doctor, with a step-by-step reasoned plan to end the war? Or Dmitri, the Soviet propaganda officer filming his fellow soldiers being killed rather than helping them? "Du hast mich gehört [you heard me]" screams a Nazi soldier at Dmitri when Dmitri fails to help him in any way, instead filming the German being wheeled off to the surgery/slaughter room with detached amoral attention. Dmitri's filming turns violence into heroism, explains Raaphorst: "When do we turn away? I don't think there is a clear answer, but that's why I wanted to push Dmitri to the level where he has to film his own comrades getting killed and eventually himself. He becomes a victim of his own propaganda you see. He becomes the subject of his own material."

The audience, me, you, we watch and can/do nothing, secretly rooting for monsters, rooting against the Soviets because of the Cold War propaganda we've been fed in Western schools, completely refusing to acknowledge the humanity of the German soldiers being hacked to pieces. This is an amoral film, which confuses people with average film expectations. The entirety of *Frankenstein's Army* is a horror – a repackaged extravagant cartoon exaggerating the most grotesque aspects of human abasement that echo fucked up things that Nazis (and the Japanese) did to ordinary human beings in the name of science and peace. At least in *Frankenstein's Army*, Dr. Frankenstein seems to have an ultimate, peaceful goal with his defilement (sort of like the United States had when it dropped the bomb on Hiroshima to "end the war"): to make the major world powers at last become allies and end the violence. "I can end the war by creating a new being that can bring them together. I can make them stop. I can make them understand each other," believes Dr. Frankenstein. "The sickness cannot be cured, so it will be cut out." The sickness is war, death, and destruction. It can only be erased through more destruction, and the construction of a final, perfect being: the final monster, a monster of peace. The irony, which is lost on Dr. Frankenstein, is that his experiments, his creations, his monsters, are all far more horrific to watch than the traditional horrors of war to which audiences, especially horror audiences, have become accustomed.

Frankenstein's Army begins with Soviet propaganda clips and the music of Mother Russia playing along. Our protagonists are Russian soldiers, entering deep into Nazi territory in the final days of the war. Dmitri, a propaganda officer, has a moving picture camera that can record sound (completely unrealistic, by the way, that type of mobile, small sound camera would not be widely available for another 15 years) and he is documenting the small group's journey as a rescue team to free Soviet P.O.W.s trapped in a Nazi stronghold. This mission is secret. When the group arrives at the camp they find it is actually a burnt church in an abandoned German village. When they venture inside, it becomes clear that there are no Soviet P.O.W.s – Dmitri is actually an agent of the Soviet Government sent to establish contact with Dr. Frankenstein and to persuade him to join the Soviet cause and share his unnatural expertise with Russia before the other Allies can get a hold of him, or before he perishes in Allied bombing. In addition, this is not actually a regular church. It's a factory, a slaughterhouse, a nightmare.

Like seriously, a nightmare. Raaphorst's twisted mind had been brewing some of the most appalling and effective monster character designs in the world since he was a child and they finally found their ultimate form as the zombots (zombie robots) in Dr. Frankenstein's underground facility. "Only the Nazis would think of something like this" exclaims soldier Sergei, "Sewing dead people together. Giving them knives for hands. It's insane." Sergei is right, it is insane. But Nazis were not the only ones who would think of something so grotesque. Viktor Frankenstein explains that the idea originally came from his father, Frankenstein Sr.: "My father said men will be more efficient if they have hammers and screwdrivers instead of fingers."

But since Viktor and Sergei are characters and not real people, the blame for this hideous idea falls on Raaphorst himself. In a 2013 interview about the DVD release of his film, Raaphorst describes where the monster designs came from:

"I've always been fascinated by *Frankenstein*. When I was a kid, my mother told me about this monster with his square head and it totally freaked me out. The square shape didn't sound logical to me, so it was really scary. My imagination took it over and started to invent cubistic monsters, which later became Transers, and then became biomechanical monsters like the ones in *FA*. Transers are my own industrial monsters I invented as a teenager. I used to dress like them and take photos. Then, when I asked myself what I wanted to make a movie about, I came up with the answer: about an army of Frankensteins. So that was it! Because I also had a deep fascination for the Second World War, I thought it might be a cool idea to combine those together. My first reaction was, "Wait a minute, you can't combine those – it's insane!" But that's exactly why I thought it would be a pretty good idea – because it was insane!"

Dr. Frankenstein himself (played stoically by Karel Roden) is completely at home among this underground facility of monsters. He blends in with ease; he is a part of it. His back-story is told by the scenes of intimate display: paintings of the Frankenstein family crest and Viktor Sr. are proudly exhibited on the walls of his study; his mother writhes in a glass case – her head has been sewn to the body of a teddy bear which bears the unmistakable spark of life that only Viktor himself can bring about. A painting of his father hangs ominously watching all. The kitchen is mundane and human; pans and coffee cups betray that Dr. Frankenstein is still very much human. Viktor was abused by his parents as a child, which is where much of his sociopathic tendencies come from. "The abused becoming the abuser and so on. Monsters are creating monsters," explains Raaphorst.

On the surface, *Frankenstein's Army* is very much a monster movie. If you scrape the surface, there's a lot more going on that perhaps the artist/filmmaker himself was not even aware of. For Raaphorst, the entirety of the piece comes together like a painting – different colors, parts of the canvas, the frame, all of that are thought of by the artist separately. The audience, however, sees it all in one form farther way and takes it all in at once. The creatures themselves are built entirely with 1945 technology; plane and engine parts, available weapons, gas masks, anything else the doctor can get his hands on, are all fair game for sewing into the flesh of his zombots. This results in monstrous things with propellers for heads, weapons for hands, and a total lack of humanity. It is a vast underground network of hundreds of corpses, all becoming Frankenstein's soldiers. The monsters are a snapshot of all that is grotesque about WWII's imagery: piles of dead bodies, barb wire, missing limbs, heavy machinery churning out weapons and bombs.

Frankenstein's Army's relentless pacing is unlike an ordinary horror film. It moves very fast from a point of view of the camera, so we see what Dmitri sees. It's the perfect mix of a horror video game and a haunted house/escape room, instead of a regular found footage horror movie. "I choose for the pacing to have the experience of falling into a rollercoaster without having the chance to contemplate the situation," says director Raaphorst. "I wanted the viewer to get pushed into the corner without thinking. I wanted the viewer to inhabit the war, like making him part of it, choosing the subjective POV instead of objective."

We don't feel like we're watching footage that was rescued, we feel like we're there while the footage is being shot. Despite the fact that we're there with Sergei, Dmitri, and the rest of the team as they wade through hell trying to make sense of senseless death and reanimation, the film is not for us. It's not about us. It's about these characters and this war. You're an observer, a peeping Tom. Unlike the flashy messes of *Van Helsing* or *Dracula Reborn*, *Frankenstein's Army* has nothing to do with your, the audience's, bullshit.

Religious iconography scatters throughout the film in a very subtle but sad way; the church's yard is filled with the bodies of burnt nuns. Statues of Jesus and The Virgin Mary lay knocked over or broken in half, covered with debris and left unloved and forgotten. One of the major criticisms that other Western nations have had of Soviet Communism is that organized religion was abolished, essentially making commies "Godless." We don't expect the soldiers to pray or appeal to God, but Sergei, upon realizing that they're all going to die in the worst and most horrible ways possible only to be reanimated as monsters, mutters, "Oh God, I'm going to hell. I am in hell." He's the best communist of the bunch, according to Dmitri, but even a good communist recognizes hell when he's there. "You can abandon religion, but you can't abandon the faith in god in the mind. I learned that soldiers could become suddenly very religious when they are facing death."

One zooms through WWII on fast-forward, through a distinctly European lens. There's a noticeable absence of American and British soldiers in *Frankenstein's Army*, something that would not have been missing in a mainstream Hollywood film. European countries have a different and more vivid legacy with WWII that Americans cannot comprehend as none of it happened on American soil. Sometimes, it seems artists and filmmakers subvert major events by creating allegories or symbolic versions of the story that are easier to comprehend to the audience than the actual event itself. "I think WWII became part of our culture," agrees Raaphorst. "Everywhere we go, we see the remains, especially in France and Germany. It always reminds us that we can't really trust human nature, and this freaks me out. It always did. You cannot rely on it. My teacher told me when I was a child that there is no generation without the experience of war. So…it's just a matter of time. This fear is the cause of my inspiration. Rather than trying to escape from it. I wanted it to research it like I think most artists would do. Exploring fears and the dark side of human nature as a way to overcome it."

Perhaps, strangely, one of the most disturbing aspects of Dr. Frankenstein's slaughterhouse/factory is the fact that his monsters have been killing and harvesting the body parts of Germans as well as Axis enemies. Frankenstein, and his Nazi experiments, is not designed to protect civilians or preserve them from further destruction. These monsters exist to enrich the power of whoever is their master. These corpses are not the safe, dried corpses of *The Texas Chainsaw Massacre II* (1986) or *Poltergeist* (1982), but the moist, plump, bloody, mutilated fresh corpses of recognizable people. It's a slaughterhouse.

The last act is pure chaos. This is why I love *Frankenstein's Army* – it makes me really, really uncomfortable. I've seen many horror films. Many, many horror films. I have written for *Bloody-Disgusting.com*, *Fangoria Magazine*, and *Famous Monsters of Filmland*, to name a few, and have reviewed countless horror movies. I see them all the time. I'm a fan. I love them. I am desensitized to violence. I was disappointed by the baby-fucking scene in *A Serbian Film* (2010). There wasn't enough baby fucking. I was let down by *Martyrs* (2008), which is supposed to be a devastating torture porn picture. Not enough torture. *Cannibal Holocaust* (1980) has some great depravity, but it's shot so poorly and honestly, I can't stand to see an animal tortured. *Human Centipede* (2009) was pretty close, I almost vomited. I know when I almost vomit that I have found what I need: a cathartic awful expression of the grotesque and horrifying. I don't want to be scared, I want to be disgusted. And not just in the mundane "oh blood and guts" way; I want to be disgusted with people, humanity, and the world. *Salo* (1975) comes close. I highly recommend the feces-eating scene at the dinner table. *The Stoning of Soraya* (2008), while not a horror movie, has come the closest to making me mentally, emotionally, and physically ill. So, apparently I am a masochist and I am always seeking extreme sensations from my horror films.

It's too late to do anything about it now, so I'll just roll with that. *Frankenstein's Army* is a steady, fast-paced, unrelenting and extremely disturbing violation of all that is holy. The unremitting onslaught of human mutilation, pain, torture, mental illness, and the combination of slaughterhouse and factory consumption of the human body is just perfect. After I watch *Frankenstein's Army*, I feel bad. I just feel unwell. I feel tense, on edge, unhappy. And it's because of this perfect tension, this fantastic sickness of images and story, that I can truly enjoy the film.

I had to know more about this film so I sought out Richard Raaphorst himself to ask him: WHY? I needed to know. I wanted to know where this horror came from and resolve why it was so fascinating to me. "I wanted to shift from entertainment into witnessing something evil or shocking," he explained, "and the border is very blurry when entertainment is delivering the opposite feeling. Very interesting how that works and why. At the time, I was merely working on instinct and not thinking in strategy and story composition. The only thing I wanted was a story that was spiraling down into madness. I was also a believer that I could make only one chance to make a movie. So I tried to get as close to my own flavor. I wanted it to be very personal rather than targeting a broad audience."

Tangled within the adrenaline-filled monster-viewing are some existential questions about war, humanity, philosophy, and insanity, as all good movies have. Dmitri forces an answer out of the doctor that seems only too obvious when he asks 'How do you make them take orders?" The doctor angrily replies, "They are puppets!" as if Dmitri's question is contemptuous and silly. Soldiers are all puppets, whether cut in half and mutilated and melded with metal and machinery or standard fully-human soldiers. They all take orders and they all kill without questioning their leaders.

The end of *Frankenstein's Army* does something very interesting; it doesn't show the ultimate culmination of violence as Sergei's head is sawed open, exposing his brain. The doctor removes half of his brain and replaces it with half of a Nazi's brain: this will bring the opposing forces together and end the war, believes Frankenstein. We do see the Nazi's head sawed open, so it is understandable why Raaphorst felt he didn't need to repeat the same gag immediately after. But still – I really wanted to see Sergei endure the bone saw fully conscious.

In the end, Dmitri has a chance to save Sergei, but he doesn't, choosing instead to film his death. Shortly after, Sacha has the opportunity to save Dmitri, but doesn't. Sacha cuts off the doctor's head and escapes into Soviet lines with his trophy, leaving Dmitri to perish in the bombings. It's a downer ending, sort of, if you like Dmitri. Dmitri is not likeable, however, so I always root for his death. Sacha is a little shit though. Sergei is the only sympathetic character in the entire film; an occupied nationality thrust into a war of defense against the Nazis. Sergei would have saved Dmitri had it been the other way around, I truly believe it.

"I think in an American Hollywood version, he would have saved him, or even sacrifice his own life for him," explains Raaphorst about Sacha and Dmitri. "I don't think this should happen in real life at all."

Fuck the American Hollywood version. Raaphorst's take on truth and violence is refreshingly pessimistic. He manages to tear up nationalism, duty, friendship, empathy, and a sense of wholeness from not only the individual, but also from the audience and the general state of the world at large. Perhaps that's what really makes me feel so ill when I watch the movie. Or maybe it's just the people cut-in-half with propellerheads. Both are pretty upsetting...in a good way.

ALIEN
BY
GREGORY S. BURKART

Writer/Producer/Composer
Tales from the Netherweb, Blumhouse.com, Fangoria,
FEARnet, Bloody Disgusting, Dread Central
Facebook: @Gregory.Burkart
Twitter: @G9Burkart Instagram: @G9Creative

There are many truly brilliant horror films, and a select group of these are undisputed classics of the genre. But above this lofty list, there lives a mere handful of genre movies so iconic, so unforgettable, they transcend the spheres of art and entertainment to become something far greater – something so deeply ingrained into modern culture that even those who have never actually seen the film will recognize certain moments, images and sounds instantly. *Jaws* and *The Exorcist* are more than just classics – they're terrifying touchstones in history, and nearly everyone can identify them from the tiniest fragments of sight and sound.

But while I love them all (well, most of them), no horror

film has wormed its way into my DNA as thoroughly and intimately as Ridley Scott's 1979 classic *Alien*. Many have come close (John Carpenter's *The Thing* comes to mind), but no single film has matched the life-shaking impact of seeing *Alien* for the first time – on a giant movie screen, with nothing to protect my young self (besides my occasionally interlaced fingers) from the awesome spectacle playing out before me – and I mean "awesome" in the most literal sense, as defined in the dictionary: "extremely impressive or daunting; inspiring great admiration, apprehension, or fear."

To me, even four decades after it first hit movie screens, *Alien* was, is, and always shall meet every one of those criteria.

I'll never forget my first taste of *Alien* in the Spring of 1979: I was in a theater with my father, attending another movie (ironically, I have no recollection of the film we were about to watch). When the coming attractions began, I found myself propelled through a starfield to the accompaniment of dissonant electronic soundscapes. Naively, I thought perhaps I was about to see a trailer for *Star Trek: The Motion Picture*, which was slated for release that December.

But as the score grew darker and more ominous (years later, I would learn this was an excerpt from an album by composer Isao Tomita, whom Ridley Scott originally considered to score the film itself), I quickly realized I was in for something very different.

That's the "apprehension" part of the definition above – which kicked in around the same time the camera revealed a rough-surfaced gray egg, nested in a sandy bed symbolizing the surface of a barren world. At the top of the screen, a series of abstract, glyph-like symbols assembled into letters: I was about to encounter something A-L-I-E-N.

By the time the title had locked into place, the egg suddenly cracked open, releasing a strobing green glow – and that horrifying, unearthly screech (the first element of Alien to embed itself into the cultural zeitgeist), like a scream from the void. I could actually hear my heart thud against my ribcage in shock.

But the horror had just begun. A rapid-fire montage of intense scenes from the film – intercut with hand-held shots of Sigourney Weaver as Ripley, running at top speed through the claustrophobic corridors of the *Nostromo* – assaulted my senses. What is she running from? Where is all this happening? What the hell is that thing? The trailer had no narration (which was rather uncommon for the '70s), and offered no answers to my questions apart from the title itself – accompanied by that same nightmare-inducing screech, and concluding with the scariest tagline I'd ever read:

"In Space No One Can Hear You Scream."

This is where that "great admiration and fear" part kicked in: my young mind had never before wrestled with both of those emotions at the same time – and it was almost more than I could bear. I was completely terrified by what I'd just witnessed, and yet I immediately turned to my dad (who shared my love of science fiction) and asked if we could see *Alien* when it came to our town.

"Are you sure you can handle it?" he asked, clearly aware how scared I was. I could only nod silently in response. Being quite conservative in his tastes, he said he would have to learn more about the movie first, as it was rated R and off-limits without his approval.

Being about a century before the internet, we had to wait for a review to come out...but fortunately, less than a week later, Siskel & Ebert's Sneak Previews (back when it originally aired on PBS) reviewed the film, and the critics lavished it with praise, tagging it as one of their favorites of the year to date – and possibly one of the best science fiction movies ever made.

The review was accompanied by short excerpts from the film, including the nail-biting scene of Captain Dallas (Tom Skerritt) crawling through the *Nostromo*'s uncomfortably narrow air shafts, sweating profusely in the heat of a very real flamethrower, tracking something unseen but obviously deadly...and discovering it's now tracking him.

Watching these scenes on our 21-inch console TV slightly reduced the scope of the film's cosmic horror, misleading me into thinking "maybe it's not as scary as the trailer," and convincing Dad it was acceptable for me to watch – but with one stern caveat.

"Don't blame me if you have nightmares," he said.

"It's just a movie," I replied. But those words weren't really directed at him...I was trying to fortify myself against what I would soon experience on a giant screen.

Finally, *Alien* arrived at one of the largest movie houses in town. Mind you, this was before the age of the multi-screen cineplex or the home video revolution – when theatrical releases brought maximum spectacle in order to get butts off the couch and into the theater.

By then, my tension level was already high, having been juiced by curious peeks at movie tie-in books and magazine articles – in which I finally got a glimpse of the title beast, designed by an artist I'd never heard of named H.R. Giger. His concepts looked like he had somehow fallen asleep on a blank canvas and awakened with his most horrific dreams magically imprinted on it. I'd also been fed wide-eyed tales of the film's scariest and bloodiest moments by friends lucky enough to have caught a preview screening – including that scene, which made *Alien* infamous for generations to come.

From these brief but potent introductions, I knew I was in for the experience of a lifetime – even if I paid dearly for it with a full summer's worth of nightmares.

As the ticket line stretched around the block, I began to realize I was part of a very special club: people whose collective fascination had driven them to this place, even as they chattered nervously about the monsters lurking inside that projection booth, waiting to be unleashed.

With my dad at my side, and our seats just far enough from the screen to keep some kind of psychological distance, I settled in nervously – still trying to convince myself that *Alien* was nothing but a movie, populated by actors just pretending to be scared, and Giger's monstrous creations were only models, puppets and probably some guy in a rubber suit (although that defense didn't prevent me from being terrified by a TV viewing of The Creature from the Black Lagoon a few years earlier).

But any trace of fortitude went out the door when the 20th Century Fox logo segued into a slow pan across an unknown world, to the accompaniment of surreal, unearthly wailing (which I later learned was achieved by a musician blowing through a conch shell, with heavy reverb added). My chances of escaping this movie unscathed were instantly dashed.

Obviously, I don't need to recap the events of the film; it's quite likely if you're reading this essay, you've seen *Alien* at least once (although I'm going to guess you've seen it many more times than that). Suffice to say, *Alien* is a film of moments – each of which is part of something far greater than a mere motion picture.

Those moments are many: the landing party's first look at the alien craft and the "Space Jockey" within; Kane's (John Hurt) fateful encounter with the egg (I can still hear the theater audience screaming at him not to put his face so close to that gloppy mess inside); the near-silent hunt for the "facehugger" in the medical lab; the first revelation of the fully-grown creature as it descends upon Brett (Harry Dean Stanton); Dallas's aforementioned crawl through the air shaft; Ripley's desperate run for the shuttle as "Mother," the ship's computer, impassively counts down the seconds before the *Nostromo* self-destructs... but of course, I'm saving the film's most iconic, heart-stopping scenes for last.

I'd already heard detailed descriptions from my friends about Kane's sudden, horrifying death...but nothing I'd concocted in my imagination could compare to Hurt's portrayal of Kane's spasms of agony as he's surrounded by his increasingly panicked shipmates – who have no idea what's happening inside him.

When that hideous pink thing erupted from Kane's chest,

hundreds of audience members screamed their lungs out. I wasn't sure if the birth of the "chestburster" or the crowd's shrieks of terror and revulsion scared me more...all I know is I could feel my entire body lift about two inches from my seat, and I swear my heart stopped beating for at least two seconds, causing the world to turn gray before my eyes, before it began frantically pounding again, bringing me back to some semblance of consciousness.

I sat back in breathless shock, barely noticing other people leaving the theater, unable to endure what they'd just witnessed. My father, surely thinking he'd made a bad call allowing me to see this movie, glanced over at me in concern. I gave him a silent look and crooked smile that communicated all he needed to know: I was in this race to the finish, no matter the consequences.

But *Alien* wasn't through with me. Not by a long shot.

As those moments played out, I could sense the tension building in the audience again: people were muttering, whispering, even faintly whimpering...until another wave of screams was released when the once-small creature revealed itself as an eight-foot-tall, jet-black manifestation of Giger's nightmares made flesh (or whatever slime-oozing matter it was composed of), making short work of poor Brett and retreating into the shadows.

More people left the theater after that...and then a few more when Dallas made his ill-fated crawl through the cramped air ducts. As Lambert (Veronica Cartwright) shouts into her headset, "It's moving right towards you!" and the stoic Captain finally loses his composure and begins to panic, I'll admit I almost reached my own breaking point.

I kept silently repeating that mantra: It's only a movie. But there was still plenty more movie left to watch...and even in my naïve youth, I knew the filmmakers were saving up something terrifying enough to knock me down for good.

When the film's second-biggest shock arrived, I'd expected it to come in the form of another attack from that hideous space-monster – and so, apparently, had the audience, as their resulting explosion of shrieks indicated.

Instead, the attack came from within the crew itself – in the form of Science Officer Ash (Ian Holm), whom I'd already suspected was up to no good; but along with nearly everyone in that theater, I had absolutely no idea Ash was not even a human being – until, of course, he begins sweating a milky substance and attacks Ripley while uttering bizarre animal grunts.

After Parker (Yaphet Kotto) rushes to Ripley's aid and strikes Ash in the head with a fire extinguisher, Ash has what can only be described as the most horrifying seizure depicted on film (and having experienced a grand mal seizure firsthand, I can tell you they're about the scariest thing the human brain can come up with). During this scene, the entire audience had been watching in tense silence; to me, it felt like that gut-twisting weightlessness I'd experienced on my first rollercoaster ride, when the car reached the top of its highest peak.

Then came the inevitable plunge, as I witnessed something my already-tormented mind just couldn't grasp: Parker's second strike literally knocks Ash's head off.

The audience went crazy. I swear I saw one person faint dead away, their forehead rebounding off the seat in front of them. If what I'd just beheld on the screen hadn't shocked me senseless, I'm sure I would have laughed. Laughter finally did sweep through the crowd a few moments later, building in volume as they reeled from the utter absurdity of the scene. I wasn't laughing along, though – I was mortified. Did I really just see that?

I could feel myself sinking deeper and deeper into my seat...but still determined to go the distance. You can survive this, I told myself. My father kept one eye on me, though, and I'm sure I wasn't doing a great job of hiding my trepidation as the alien continued to polish off the rest of the crew.

As Ripley, the sole human survivor, races against the destruct countdown, I was right there with her – and although I'd never once looked at my watch during the movie to see how much time had transpired, I knew the finish line was in sight. It had to be. The human mind couldn't hold much more terror than this.

The filmmakers, in their sadistic genius, knew that too – and that's why they saved one more huge scare for the finale. Oddly enough, at the moment the alien jumps out at Ripley from its hiding place in the shuttle, I didn't react quite as violently as I had before; looking back, I think I'd reached the limits of sensory overload. But when Ripley triumphs at last, blasting the creature to atoms with the ship's engines, I suddenly felt a surge of throat-clenching emotion: not fear (finally), but the exhilaration of having survived. I imagine the look on my face at that moment was nearly identical to that of Sigourney Weaver as she watches her adversary fly away in a cloud of plasma: overwhelming relief, of course, but mixed with an intense melancholy: in Ripley's case, for the loss of her shipmates; but for me, it was the realization that it was all over... and I wanted more.

As the strains of Howard Hanson's Symphony No. 2 swelled on the soundtrack, I felt one last surprise, triggering a lump in my throat and a faint trace of tears: not only had I survived the most terrifying film I'd ever seen, but I wanted to see it all over again. Immediately.

My first viewing of *Alien* was more than just two hours of entertainment – it was a gift, a treasure, a transcendent experience I've never forgotten. I can still picture the theater, smell the popcorn, hear the shouts of terror (as it turns out, in a theater everyone can hear you scream) and tension-breaking laughter. I can still see my dad's watchful eye looking in my direction, and hear his final comment to me as the credits crawled.

"That was intense," he said, in his usual soft-spoken, stoic manner. But his eyes asked a silent question: "Was it worth it?"

My own wordless reply came in the form of a smile – a full, genuine one this time – and Dad looked relieved. To him, a man of simple pleasures and a love for sci-fi, it was just a fun, scary monster movie...but I think he understood *Alien* was much, much more than that to me.

Alien was also the launching point that set me on the path to create wild, amazing and frightening stories of my own. I hope one day to recapture that precious lightning – that genuine sense of awe – and bring it to life before a stunned, terrified, amazed and delighted audience.

By the way, Dad, if you're listening up there: I never had a single nightmare about the movie. Hell, why would I? I had just confronted the ultimate cosmic horror and survived...then returned to that experience again and again.

Even now, I still feel that surge of exhilaration and melancholy as *Alien*'s end titles roll.

TALES FROM THE CRYPT PRESENTS:
DEMON KNIGHT
BY
GRAHAM DENMAN

Director
Greenlight
Instagram: @GrahamFromTheCrypt
Facebook: @Graham.Denman.16 Twitter: @KillingTimeGD

December, 1994. I was a nine-year-old kid walking through the Mann Theater lobby in my hometown of Agoura Hills, California (where I practically lived whenever I wasn't at Blockbuster staring at horror VHS covers, or Pee Wee Comics picking up the latest issue of *Spawn*, or the TILT arcade at the Fallbrook Mall playing *Mortal Kombat 2* and *Killer Instinct*). I'll never forget coming across a slime green, neon purple poster for *Tales from the Crypt*'s upcoming first feature film *DEMON KNIGHT*! The film would come out a month later on January 13th, but when I saw that poster with the Crypt Keeper's giant face while Billy Zane, surrounded by demons, pointed at me, I knew I had to see it. Sadly, that day didn't come for some time, specifically, over a year later when it finally wound up on HBO. One night in my room, there it was. I could not believe my eyes, I was finally going to witness this thing in action. And let me tell you, it did not disappoint. The creature effects, Billy Zane's AMAZING performance (let's be honest, his best), the camera work (more on that in a moment) and the beautiful gel-lit scenery. It was everything I wanted and more. Most people probably would never dare say this, but *Demon Knight* changed my life. Yes, you read that correctly. To this day, it is still my favorite horror film.

Here are a few reasons why.

So, remember when I mentioned the camera work? How could you not? I only mentioned it moments ago. Anyhow, in the early '90s there was a tone, look, and feel that was very specific in films and commercials: Dutch angles, wide angle lenses, and an insane color palette (mainly green and purple for advertising; *Tales From The Crypt*, *Goosebumps*, *Spawn*, Nickelodeon...you get the point). I was always attracted to this style of filming for some reason as a youngster - it just felt like things popped out of the screen.

It turns out that some of my favorite *TFTC* episodes and the amazing *House On Haunted Hill* remake from 1999 directed by Bill Malone all share one thing in common: cinematographer Rick Bota. All of these things I love were shot by the same guy! NO WONDER they all felt similar in ways! Ernest Dickerson, the director behind *Demon Knight* as well as films like *Juice, Bulletproof, Bones* (yeah, the Snoop Dogg flick) and multiple episodes of *The Walking Dead*, was a fantastic cinematographer in his own right. He and Bota made an incredible pair for *Demon Knight*. Every scene felt like it had been visually ripped out of the EC Comics universe and they understood what it was at all times. You could feel the fun they were having through the screen.

As for *Demon Knight*'s story, it's a classic siege scenario. People are trapped in a building. Demons are trying to get in, what more do you need? Well, most films like this don't exactly have GREAT scripts or characters attached to them, however, *Demon Knight* truly does have both of those things in my opinion. The story centers around the film's McGuffin, a key filled with the blood of Jesus Christ that can keep the demons away and save the world from total darkness. Brayker, played by William Sadler, is in charge of said blood key and must help save an all-star cast featuring Thomas Haden Church, Dick Miller, C.C.H. Pounder, Gary Farmer, Charles Fleischer and (pre-Will Smith) Jada Pinkett, all of whom are wonderfully cast. The dialogue is so well put together for a horror flick and nearly every set piece is executed to perfection. *Demon Knight* is the kind of film you should seek out if you are tired of the same old mainstream horror movies being pumped into cinemas because the flick genuinely holds up to this day as a highlight in not only '90s horror cinema but of the genre as a whole.

As a director, I aspire to someday make a horror film even half as good as this fun film ride. The original script didn't even have actual demons in it if you can believe it. It started out as a story about satanic door-to-door salesmen and eventually was re-written to appeal to a more horror-friendly environment.

So, why did *Demon Knight* change my life? It was one of those movies that just happened at the right place and right time for me. It exposed me to a side of horror I had yet to see at that time. Sure, it was scary, but it was just so goddamned entertaining, funny, and thrilling. I can't even tell you how many times I have seen *Demon Knight*. Hell, one of my biggest Bluray dreams was to see a proper transfer loaded with special features and a commentary track someday. Guess what? Scream Factory answered my prayers a few years ago. It also taught me a lot about how to make your audience care about your characters in a horror film without making them all feel one dimensional. I mean, sure, there are tons of great horror films with well rounded characters in them, but you have to remember this film affected me at a time where I had not seen a lot of that. Mostly, I just feel it's a highly underrated film. Shortly after, a "sequel" called *Bordello Of Blood* was released that had abso-lutely no ties to *Demon Knight* other than the Crypt Keeper wrap-around and a cameo for the blood key. Honestly, I try to forget it.

With that being said, *Demon Knight* is my favorite because it has all the ingredients needed for a damned good time at the movies as well as being one of the last great practical ef-fects-heavy films in horror prior to the takeover of CGI. Walter Phelan (who you may also know as Dr. Satan in *House Of 1000 Corpses*), was one of the film's demons and he once told me all the work that went into creating those creatures. The suits - the movement - the performance. Fascinating stuff.

If you ever do pick up the Blu-ray, I highly recommend watching the making-of featurette. It's full of so many great stories and behind-the-scenes info that offer a look into why this film is so special.

As a director, I have always dreamed of making a sequel if Dickerson himself didn't want to do it because, if it were not for *Demon Knight*, I would not have some of the style and tone to my films. I owe *Demon Knight*, Ernest Dickerson and Rick Bota a lot of gratitude for teaching me how to light a scene, create tension or suspense with my lenses/angles and, most of all, how to add a pinch of fun to the horror at hand. *Demon Knight* is not just a horror film. It's a time capsule of where I came from, who I have become, and why I love film in the first place. The days of seeing films like *Demon Knight* in theaters around the world are sadly behind us, but they still are out there, waiting to be seen by new eyes to form new ideas. If you can't smile at Billy Zane's insane turn as The Collector or admire the practi-cal effects on display in this film then what's the point of being a horror fan? We all became horror fans because there was a movie at some point in our lives that stopped us in our tracks and changed how we viewed the genre.

So, "you bunch of ho-dunk po-dunk well-then-there-moth-erfuckers" should revisit *Demon Knight* as soon as possible or watch it for your first time you can take a trip back to 1995 when crazy films with crazy ideas took crazy chances and were crazy fun. It's truly been an honor to write this piece for this book, so thank you for taking the time to read my passion for this film. It all started with a green and purple poster. Here we are nearly 25 years later and I just wrote about *Demon Knight*, my favorite horror movie...while that poster hangs on the wall behind me.

NIGHT OF THE LIVING DEAD
(1968)
BY
CHELSEA STARDUST

Director
All That We Destroy, Satanic Panic, Slashed! The Musical
Twitter: @StardustChelsea
Instagram: @ChelseaStardust

I'm frequently asked, "What is the horror film that made you want to direct horror films?" Without hesitation, I always answer George A. Romero's *Night Of The Living Dead*. My relationship with this incredible film dates back to 1995, when I was 10 years old, but more on that in a moment.

My dad, an artist and cinefile, is responsible for my love of horror cinema (and all cinema in general). I was raised on the Universal Classic Monster movies. Tod Browning's *Dracula* was and has always been my favorite, with *The Wolfman, Creature From The Black Lagoon* and *Frankenstein* close behind. I would watch those films every October, usually while my mom, dad and I would clean and carve pumpkins for our annual

Halloween party. Halloween was a big deal in my family, bigger than Christmas. We celebrated Halloween throughout the whole month of October, a tradition I still carry on to this day.

One year, my dad decided I was old enough to see one of his favorite horror films, *Night Of The Living Dead*. The title of the film was disturbing enough, let alone the black, white and red VHS box he handed to me (which I still have). "If you get too scared we can turn it off." Well, in my 10-year-old brain, that became a little challenge. I could handle this movie! Besides, all of the Universal Monster movies where in black and white and I could handle all of those, no problem.

How naïve I was.

He popped the VHS tape into our player and that unsettling opening score instantly sank into my bones and took hold. I was terrified and we weren't even 2 minutes into the film. Nothing had even happened yet! But I immediately knew this film was NOT like the monster movies I had seen so many times. I watched as two young, dapper siblings arrive at cemetery…but it's broad daylight so it should be fine…right? Wrong. Johnny taunts Barbara with his famous "They're coming to get you, Barbara. They're coming for you, Barbara! They're coming for you! Look, there comes one of them now!" And suddenly zombie Bill Heinzman attacks Barbara and Johnny! Although Barbara manages to escape, I was shocked at Johnny's death. We just met him, how could he be dead already? (Keep in mind I hadn't seen *Psycho* yet, so killing off a lead character so early in a film was completely foreign to me).

My dad glanced over at me and asked, "You okay?" I was hypnotized and terrified, but I wasn't going to let my dad know that, so I managed to squeak out a "yes." For the next 90 minutes, I was completely possessed by the film. The creepy score, haunting cinematography, beautiful lighting, and of course Duane Jones' incredible performance as Ben. And the dead… they just kept coming. When Karen attacks, murders and then eats her mother Helen, I was horrified. I had never seen anything like that, especially from a little girl like myself. It felt like this night of terror was never going to end for the occupants of that little white farmhouse. It also seemed like this film was preparing me for survival, almost like a guide on how to make it through an undead attack. I took lots of mental notes should I ever need these survival skills in the future.

The ending of the film completely devastated me.

Ben was a handsome, no-nonsense, take-charge man. He was not to be fucked with and was going to do whatever it took to survive this nightmare. When the sun came up and the horrific night finally came to an end, Ben was the only survivor in the house. I was relieved when I saw he was still alive, but in a matter of minutes he's gunned down by the local police and good old boys who assume he's one of the living dead. Then, over the end credits, these men jab his body with meat hooks, drag him onto a pile of dead bodies and set them on fire. I was in total shock. I remember being so upset my eyes filled with tears. I think my dad was worried that maybe I was too young for the film, but I told him that even though I was a mess of emotions, I was completely in love with the movie. I remember watching it again the next day with my babysitter.

It wasn't until I was a teenager that I fully comprehended the racial implications of the ending, but even as a small child I knew what I was witnessing was horrible and wrong. To this day the ending of this film still destroys me.

I watch *Night Of The Living Dead* every October, either the same VHS copy that inspired me to become a horror film director or the beautiful Criterion Collection Blu-ray. However, I cannot watch this film alone, especially at night, for fear that the living dead might come for me...

CANDYMAN
BY
SEAN KELLER

Screenwriter/Songwriter
All That We Destroy, The Capture,
Giallo, Slashed! The Musical
Instagram: @RevSeanK Twitter: @_SeanKeller

A screen pulses with hundreds of bees.
A hauntingly deep voice reverberates.
"They will say that I have shed innocent blood.
What's blood for, if not for shedding?"
It's chill-inducing.
Every time.

The first time I saw *Candyman* was during its theatrical release in 1992 in Washington, D.C. Back then, I was a snobby young film nut in denial about being a horror fan. Even worse, I was a musician, which in D.C. was supposed to be very serious business. I was into indie bands and art-house movies. I dated activists and wanna-be poets. I drank black coffee and rolled my own smokes and had my head firmly stuck up my ass about what constituted art. Horror wasn't art. Maybe, back when Kubrick or Polanski made it. But since the slashers? Nah.

But from the opening pipe organ and choir score by Philip Glass, it was obvious to me that *Candyman* was more than just another horror film. It was mythic. Romantic. Brutal. And it was something else, something transgressive. It might even be a work of art. I remember going to a mid-afternoon screening and emerging from the theater alone into the early-autumn night thrilled and titillated, but also creeped-the-fuck-out. I was twenty-three years old - too old to be scared by a movie, right? But it got me.

Candyman is an inspired tale of urban dread in which folklore and myth rise from America's history of racial violence to create a regal, African-American, hook-handed killer whose power comes from others' belief in him. Candyman is as gothic and iconic as any of the Universal monsters, but unlike the chaste and restrained black & white creatures of the past, Candyman is bathed in blood and filed with a raw, sexual power.

There is a cautionary tale at the center of the film that echoes the Neitzche quote "if you gaze long enough into an abyss, the abyss will gaze back into you." Virginia Madsen's Helen is a grad student researching a local urban legend, hoping to be published. She is smart, charming, and very easy to root for (especially when sharing the screen with Kasi Lemmons' sweet, but cautious Bernadette). The two of them are a solid team on the path to a dissertation, but when they are belittled by male academic gatekeepers, Helen's ambition and hu bris pushes them deeper into danger than either of them would otherwise be willing to go. It is Helen's pride as much as her academic curiosity that leads to her doom. It is the mere act of digging into the myth that gives Candyman strength. She calls upon him. She wills him into her life. When she finds herself backed into a corner with all hope lost, she calls Candyman's name again, this time to kill for her. From that moment on,

Helen is linked to the monster. She is culpable. She is complicit. She has become the darkness. It is a character turn you rarely see in cinema and it feels dirty, like illicit sex; like something perverted you shouldn't be watching. And sitting there in the cinema, it felt like something I might accidentally take home with me in a filthy, dark corner of my subconscious. Believe me, there was no fucking way I was going to say "Candyman" in the mirror five times that night.

The dread I felt was due in large to director Bernard Rose's commitment to reality. I know that may sound odd in reference to what is essentially a retelling of the Bloody Mary urban legend, but despite its supernatural trappings, *Candyman* is super-fucking-scary because it's incredibly real. Maybe too real. Every casting choice rings of authenticity. Every character seems lived-in. The university setting is flawlessly banal because it's shot on location, as is the centerpiece of the film, Cabrini Green, a Chicago housing project seemingly abandoned to crime and decay. Rose adapted Clive Barker's source material (a short story called *The Forbidden*) specifically for this location because its graffitied and crumbling towers instantly raised the stakes of the film. It is a place of real danger and real shame. In Rose's hands, this monument to the failed economic policies of an inherently racist society becomes analogous to the turreted castles of the classics. Cabrini Green is the dark threshold across which our hero must venture and where evil lurks. Its use in *Candyman* creates a visual language for a new Urban Gothic, far from *Rosemary's Baby*'s posh Upper West Side. And once again, it's way too real.

There is, of course, the over-the-fucking-top-way-too-real fact that Rose hypnotized Virginia Madsen repeatedly during filming, which you can see in scenes where she's in Candyman's thrall. Madsen doesn't blink, but her pupils dilate as tears stream. She seems like she's under a spell because she is quite literally under the director's spell. It's unnerving to watch, and honestly, abusive behavior by a director. The overall effect in the film, however, is stunning. The layering of tactile reality in scene after scene creates a framework that carries the unreality and allows *Candyman* to transcend artifice and emerge as art. The film is full of art. Candyman himself was an artist; a portrait painter. And the most iconic bit of art in the film is a mural of Candyman on the wall of a heavily vandalized apartment, through which Helen climbs, seemingly from Candyman's open mouth.

And then there's Tony Todd. What a fucking performance. His Candyman is a bold new monster. A creature both grand and horrific. Sexy and menacing. With a fur-trimmed coat and a voice that is (appropriately) the stuff of legend, Todd is the embodiment of taboo. A stately black man with a huge phallic hook making a blonde white woman his puppet? Twenty-seven years later, I'm still unpacking all of that. Tony Todd not only delivers a tragic, vengeful monster for the ages, he does it with a mouthful of bees! Real live bees! This movie is too fucking real for its own good!

There is a condition among young snobbish men that denies greatness to anything contemporary, and I for-fucking-sure fell for that shit. I knew *Candyman* was really good when I saw it, but I didn't think it was great. It was new. New things can't be great. The second time I saw it, a year later on VHS, I thought maybe it was kinda great, but no classic. Years later, I knew it was a classic, but not top five material. And so on, and so on.

Now, as a horror screenwriter, *Candyman* is a film I aspire to and return again and again to for inspiration. It perfectly blends story and performance with score and makeup effects to create a hauntingly effective horror film. It is a masterclass in layering myth into story, without losing the sense of a specific time and place. I watched the DVD over and over when I made the decision to write my first feature screenplay (a regrettably awful thing that will not be named) as a reminder of how elegant horror can be...and how far away from it I was.

Most importantly, *Candyman* gave me hope in horror. It made me believe horror could be inspiring and thoughtful. It drove me into a deeper connection to the genre. And this genre has given me creative life.

Every time I watch *Candyman*, it climbs in my estimation. I can't think of any other film I can honestly say that about. Year by year, *Candyman* has climbed my list of favorites, breaking into the top five and then overtaking *Alien*, *The Thing*, and even my beloved *Night of the Living Dead* to officially rank as my favorite horror film.

Watch it again with the lights down and the sound way up. You'll thank me.

HALLOWEEN II (1981)

BY
DOUGLAS TAIT

Actor/Producer
Hellboy (2019), *Annabelle Comes Home, Teen Wolf, Grimm*
Instagram: @ActorDouglasTait Twitter: @DouglasTait
Facebook: @TheCreatureMan

My favorite holiday growing up was Halloween. I would typically spend weeks dressing up our house to graciously provide trick-or-treaters the scare of their life on Halloween night. I would also plan out my costume months in advance. My mom custom-made my elaborate wardrobe on her Singer sewing machine. No generic Kmart costumes for me, I demanded film quality! I passionately loved monsters and dressing up to scare kids. During the 1980s, my parents bought us our first VCR at Fedco, in Van Nuys, CA. The VCR had been returned, and inside was a VHS tape of *Halloween II*.

When I initially spotted the tape, I didn't know anything about the acclaimed movie. I assumed it was a film dedicated to my favorite holiday. I was with my sitter when I popped it in for the first time. From the moment it began, I sat entranced. I watched as Laurie Strode emotionally tells the kids to call the police, and they leave screaming in frantic terror. I watched carefully as Michael stalks his sister in luminous darkness. I eagerly watched as Dr. Loomis delivers his powerful bone chilling lines: I shot him six times! I shot him in the heart-but... HE'S NOT HUMAN!

I was instantly hooked on this film. I was in complete awe over Michael Myers, the eerie music, and the entire film. It was so frightening to me, but I couldn't get enough of it. I viewed it again and again. I invited my friends from school over to experience this new film I discovered. I recorded John Carpenter's chilling *Halloween* score off the poor quality speakers of my television. I would play the music and slowly creep around the house as my favorite villain, Michael Myers. I had to be Michael for Halloween that year! At the time, there weren't multiple options for masks. Don Post was the King of masks and I owned several of them, but I couldn't find the Myers masks at my local Halloween store. There was no Amazon Prime in the '80s, kids! My dad had a pair of old mechanic coveralls, and mom tailored them to fit me. I found a suitable pair of worn-out boots at the local thrift store, but nevertheless, we couldn't find the sacred mask. I ended up using my mom's old ratty wig and painted my face white. It looked hilarious, but I owned that character on Halloween night!

Something about the performance of Dick Warlock has stuck with me ever since. The graceful movements Dick gave to Michael Myers undoubtedly influenced my performances over the years. You can witness it with the Dread Doctor character I played on Season 5 of the TV series *Teen Wolf*. When I started to play characters in special effects makeup and masks, I would dream about portraying Myers. I portrayed the iconic Jason Voorhees in the ending scene of *Freddy vs. Jason*, but I wasn't a fan of the *Friday The 13th* franchise like I was with *Halloween*. In 2015, my dream almost came true. Thanks to my good buddy Sean Clark, I had a meeting with Malek Akkad and Ryan

Freimann for the role of Michael Myers in *Halloween Returns*. Patrick Melton and Marcus Dunstan were the screenwriters on the film, and Marcus was directing. Everything looked promising, and I enjoyed a lengthy talk with Malek about my love for the franchise. I explained to him how thrilling it was to be considered for this role, and how much his dad (Moustapha Akkad's) film meant to me growing up. Malek, Marcus, and I were all in agreement about the character and the film. I put on the mask in front of them and performed the walk, and a chill went throughout my body, it felt surreal. Unfortunately, for whatever reason, the movie fell through. Every October 31st I play the original *Halloween* score and reminisce about watching that film as a child. I loved the most recent *Halloween* film. I genuinely felt like it accurately captured the essence of the first two *Halloween* films. I'm nevertheless hoping that someday I will get the opportunity to portray the iconic character that instantly began my passionate love of horror films. It is on my bucket list!

LAIR OF THE WHITE WORM
BY
COURTNEY & HILLARY ANDUJAR

Production Designer/Directors
Scare Package, Girl on the Third Floor, The Wind, Bloodline
Instagram: (Courtney): @PittaSnakes
Instagram (Hillary): @2_Decadent
Andujar-Twins.com

B ased on Bram Stoker's widely hated* final novel inspired by the British legend of the Lambton Worm, *Lair of the White Worm* has everything: mystical archeology, seduction & silk sheets, dangerous bubble baths, hypnotism, excessive tea pouring, idiot cops, tanning beds, and phallic relics... it's no surprise that Ken Russell—a man who lived for artistic license—was drawn to this story and went totally rogue in his adaptation, mashing-up different symbolism and folklore into a sleazy, lush kaleidoscope of the subconscious.

Russell relentlessly incorporates snake imagery, both literal (on currency, as a giant parade costume, in real life and in dream sequences, on the board game Snakes and Ladders, in a crossword puzzle, and in numerous works of art across many mediums) and metaphorical (hoses, tubes, plates of spaghetti). The audience is "snake watching" along with Lady Sylvia. As a counterpart to all this phallic imagery, there's unabashed female sexuality and definitely a stocking fetish. Russell manages to give a close up to nearly every woman's garters, even those on the Trent girls' dying mother.

Ken Russell thrives at casting, and this film is no exception. A young Hugh Grant debuts in his first and last horror film as the revered Lord James D'Ampton; Oscar winner Peter Capaldi gives a bizarrely compelling performance as the archaeologist Angus Flint; Yugoslavian royalty Catherine Oxenberg is the innocent Eve Trent; Sammi Davis, who slays in Allison Anders' segment of *Four Rooms*, plays Eve's tomboy sister; and, of course, Amanda Donahoe is divine as the temptress of knights, Lady Sylvia Marsh.

Lady Sylvia, who uses her looks and wits to seduce and disarm potential sacrifices for the fabled snake, has all the makings of an iconic villainess. She lives a delightfully hedonistic lifestyle, drinking whiskey and playing board games in her opulent mansion. Her wardrobe is wild: thigh-high patent leather heels in what would seem like every color, négligés, and geometric framed sunglasses. Her demeanor is cool and uncrackable, and her dialog is entertainingly savage.

Lord D'Ampton: "Do you have children?"
Lady Sylvia Marsh: "Only when there are no men around."

She does her best to corrupt the Trent sisters. ("Poor little virgins, masturbating in the dark," she mutters.) Lady Sylvia's charms are so irresistible, it's impossible not to root for her.

Music is a weapon in the story, hypnotizing snakes and those they've possessed. When teenage hitchhiker Kevin plays his harmonica, Lady Sylvia scolds him: "That sort of music freaks me out." Thank goodness for the record with exotic snake charming tunes Lord D'Ampton's father picked up from a belly dancer in Istanbul. The score is a sultry mix of saxophone and synths with a lively original folk song about the D'Ampton worm.

Even after being barraged with insane sets and scenarios in the first part of the film, nothing could prepare us for the finale, which literally kicks off when Hugh Grant slices a woman in half while doing a roundhouse kick into a drum set. The Scottish archaeologist, with an inverted cross made of blood on his cheek, exhaustedly plays bagpipes until a woozy cop falls and pops his eye out on a snake sculpture. A mongoose is deployed. I've barely closed my jaw from one instance when the next bizarre thing prompts it to drop again.

More important than the glorious third act is the surrealism throughout: the D'Ampton worm celebration feast fit for Salvador Dali with its green slime and garnished raw octopuses; the bold psychedelic interludes; the airplane dream sequence, which feels like a manifestation of David Lynch taking a handful of Zoloft and zonking out while listening to ballroom waltzes.

Intentionally or not, the film feels oddly feminist. The women are, for the most part, smarter and more powerful than the men. Lord D'Ampton hilariously never lives up to his family legacy as a snake-slayer, despite being celebrated with an annual feast where townsfolk sing about his heroism. Even when it's time for the customary virgin sacrifice, it's shockingly gender bendy, with Sylvia Marsh wearing a giant strap-on relic. And when Nurse Gladwell, with her velvety voice and slight resemblance to Marsh, nonchalantly admits to prescribing Flint the wrong antidote, we must wonder if she's in on the Lady's diabolical scheme. It feels entirely possible that this town—the same town that makes a tradition of celebrating mediocre men—is controlled by these alluring women. We'd like to think so.

---

* "The Lair of the White Worm is absolutely the most amorphous & infantile mess I've ever seen between cloth covers." - H. P. Lovecraft in a letter to Donald Wandrei, 29 Jan 1927, Mysteries of Time & Spirit

EVIL DEAD II
BY
JOSH MILLER

Writer/Producer/Director
Golan the Insatiable, Sonic the Hedgehog, 12 Deadly Days, Hey, Stop Stabbing Me!, Best Movies Never Made Podcast
Instagram: @Josh_S_Miller

What's my favorite horror movie? Think plates.

I've obsessed over so many different horror movies for different reasons at different points in my life. Watching *The Wolf Man* at the public library is what made me fall in love with monsters. Love for *Friday the 13th Part 3* was a bonding factor for one of my oldest friendships. *Scream* was the first time I felt part of the fan-swell zeitgeist on a new horror movie. *Jaws* is the film I've probably rewatched the most in my life. If I'd been asked to make a Top 5 favorite horror films list in college, the #1 slot would surely have been *The Thing* or *Re-Animator* or *The Return of the Living Dead* or *An American Werewolf in London* depending on which month you asked me. But if I'm thinking about the movie (in any genre) that had the biggest impact on me as a fan and as a filmmaker, there is really only one answer...

Evil Dead II.

The number of different memories and discoveries I associate with *ED2* is pretty epic. Even going back to before I ever watched the damned thing.

Like every horror fan of a certain age who grew up during the video store epoch, I have near mythic, rose-colored memories of strolling down the horror aisle as a kid. All those provocative VHS box covers forever burnt like a nuclear shadow into the back of my brain. *Chopping Mall. The Thing. Ghoulies. April Fool's Day. Elves. I Spit on Your Grave. Waxwork.* Tiers upon tiers of forbidden fruit! Tantalizing me, teasing me, sometimes deeply scaring me - *Scanners. Zombie. The Howling. Berserker. The Company of Wolves* - often to the point where I couldn't bring myself to even pick them up and look at the back.

Evil Dead II's cover was a combo of both. Its iconic design was both scary and almost obnoxiously alluring. I mean - those eyes! - lidlessly staring at you from a bare skull in semi-profile. Piercing, yet plaintive at the same time. At that age, I don't know that I possessed the artistic faculty to appreciate it on a design level. But unconsciously, I was responding to it big time. It's such a simple image with so much power. It sat there on the shelf like a challenge, like a colossal roller coaster I was too short to ride, but knew was my destiny to someday ride.

Thankfully this was the 1980s, so that day came maybe sooner than it should have. Like a lot of well-meaning but priority-skewed American parents of that era, my mom had a bigger issue with me watching movies with sex than she did with violence. Ironically, she didn't realize that horror movies were now riddled with more sex and nudity than most of the raunchy comedies she didn't want me renting. Bully for me and my friends (whose parents had no idea what madness my parents were letting into our eyeballs). So it was, in middle school, that I finally embarked on the VHS horror voyage of discovery.

At the time, my sister worked at a shitty strip mall video store called Panorama Video. If I agreed to hang around the store and put the returns back on the shelves, the manager let me rent four movies. And I went crazy with it. Hopped up on bulk-store candy and Mountain Dew, my friends and I would watch four horror movies almost every Saturday in my basement.

Watching movies at that age was a purer form of experience. There was no context to anything. You just took things in. For example, *Jason Takes Manhattan* was the first *Friday the 13th* movie I ever saw, after which, I proceeded to savagely devour the prior seven films in absolutely no logical order whatsoever. So it did not bother me that I hadn't seen *The Evil Dead*. For my friends and I, *ED2* was just one of the four movies we rented that night. None of them were precious. Hell, we decided the viewing order by tossing the rental cases against the couch, and whichever one fell off and hit the floor first we watched next (VHS tapes were a lot more durable than discs). These movies were merely fuel for the fire in our new ritual.

It would be great for this story if *ED2* ripped my mind open once we hit play. But I have no memory of my first viewing, other than we all enjoyed it and thought it was scary (I miss the days of being scared by everything). But something about it stayed with me, because I soon rented it again, which was rare for me with horror movies at the time.

It was this second viewing that blew my barn doors off. For one thing, I realized the movie wasn't even trying to be particularly scary. It was doing something else entirely. That first time, I was merely watching the film. Now I felt like Dr. David Bowman staring into the Monolith. I'd been shown something.

I'd known I wanted to make movies since my family got a video camera when I was in the third grade. For the most part, I understood what a director did, a writer did, etc. But Sam Raimi's kinetic, handheld camerawork made something click. It was like free jazz. It was an acting performance itself. The seemingly anarchic nature of it actually helped the filmmaking process make more sense to me - the proverbial method to the madness. Raimi's movement forced me to think about these two-dimensional images in the three-dimensional reality of a film set. It wasn't just, oh, how did they do that special effect? It was, oh, where the hell was the crew hiding if the camera just ran down that hallway and then spun around that whole room? While it would be inaccurate to say *Evil Dead II* inspired me to be a filmmaker, it most certainly inspired me to be the filmmaker I became.

I was a Raimi fanatic. I was already making home movies with our VHS camcorder - now I abandoned the tripod and took on the *ED2* style; the swooping camera moves; the extreme close-ups. I wanted to see everything Raimi made. In those hoary days before the internet, it wasn't easy. It basically came down to reading the credits on all the VHS boxes at every video store and getting lucky. Frankly, it was kind of unusual that one of the video stores in my Minnesota suburb carried *Crimewave*.

Darkman was a big movie for my group of friends. As was *Army of Darkness*. And I wore it as a badge of super coolness that I was the only one who had seen both *The Evil Dead* and *Evil Dead II* when *AOD* hit theaters, that knew this was really *Evil Dead 3*, and was thusly able to fill in everyone on what had happened before. I was the *Evil Dead* expert!

Just when my obsession with the movie had begun to wane and be replaced by other films and filmmakers, the World Wide Web and DVDs happened. As anyone who has purchased one (if not multiple) of the zillions of releases the *Evil Dead* franchise has received knows, the movies are a backstory horn-of-plenty. Learning that Raimi and company had just been scrappy Great Lakes punks making crazy home movies, just like my friends and me, absolutely legitimized (even romanticized) my own life. I absorbed it all like gospel.

Like a conspiracy nut pulling on a thread, I also pieced together a lineage between many of my favorite filmmakers at the time. Joel Coen worked as an editor on *The Evil Dead*, and Barry Sonnenfeld was the Cinematographer on the Coen Bros first three films (plus *Throw Mama From the Train, Three O'Clock High,* and *Misery).* Not to mention the discovery that Raimi shot some of the amazing second unit sequences for *The Hudsucker Proxy,* and that Bruce Campbell had a hidden cameo in *Fargo.* (Anyone else remember that bizarre published version of the *Raising Arizona* script that contained a bickering dialogue between the Coens, Raimi and Bruce Campbell as its intro??) It was like all these filmmakers I loved were drawing from the aesthetic *ED2* well. "It all makes sense now," I was mentally shouting in my dorm room.

Speaking of Bruce Campbell...I mentioned that *ED2* majorly affected me as a fan too. So no discussion of this film would be complete without mentioning Bruce.

What was The Chin's power over us?!

Where I grew up, there were no horror conventions, and I didn't get into film magazines until college (not even *Fangoria*). So, at the time, I assumed my idiot friends and I were the only Bruce fans in the world. Only we saw his genius. Normal slobs had no idea who he was. Didn't care. This was long before he appeared in Raimi's *Spider-Man* trilogy, before *Burn Notice* or *Ash vs Evil Dead*, before he did voices in *Cars 2* and *Cloudy With a Chance of Meatballs*, even before *Xena: Warrior Princess*. Along with trying to find other Raimi movies, I scoured video shelves looking for Bruce's name in credit blocks, taking whatever scraps I could find, savoring glorious turds like *Moontrap* and *Mindwarp*. I remember how stoked my friends and I were that he was in the opening of fucking *Congo* and how pissed off we were when he dies immediately.

When I got to college, I discovered two things: 1) there were other Bruce fans in the world, and 2) apparently everyone but me was already using the internet. So I quickly got myself a hotmail account, hopped on Netscape and "asked" Jeeves to find me Bruce Campbell.

Much to my shock and delight I discovered Bruce had his own website. And at a time when most celebrity websites were hideous fan-run GeoCities embarrassments, Bruce managed his website himself, and it was surprisingly great. For those who never saw the OG bruce-campbell.com, the highlight was his section of memoir style essays - short stories detailing his life in the underbelly of The Biz. And they were absolutely hilarious (he eventually turned them into the book *If Chins Could Kill.*) It was also through his site that I discovered my second-favorite website in college, fellow Raimi-verse buddy Josh Becker's BeckerFilms.com, which was as endearingly surly as Bruce's site was light and charming.

The other great feature on his site was his invitation to email him directly. Now, I'd never written a "fan letter" before. And I've never written one since. But I had to write Bruce. How could I not? He essentially asked me to! Knowing he was reading and responding to hundreds of these things a week, I wanted to keep it simple. My hotmail account is long dead, but I clearly remember that I posed to Bruce the dazzlingly erudite query: "What was your favorite scene to shoot in *Evil Dead II*?" And he responded with just two words…

"Think plates."

And I always will.

A NIGHTMARE ON ELM STREET 2: FREDDY'S REVENGE

BY
AARON MENTO

Writer/Director
Ugly Sweater Party, Standards of Living, 16 Bits
Twitter/Instagram: @AaronMento
Facebook: @Aaron.Mento

At first, I was going to write about the original *A Nightmare on Elm Street* being my favorite horror movie. Shit, it's really my favorite movie, period. I even have the Elite Limited Collector's Edition Digitally Re-Mastered Deluxe 2 Tape VHS Set right next to me, proving what a loyal fan I am. But something about this book being a sequel really inspired me to consider good old *A Nightmare on Elm Street 2: Freddy's Revenge*. But how can I even consider this? The first *Nightmare* inspired me to become a filmmaker: the screenplay is brilliant, the examination of Freddy Krueger as the id is fascinating (hurray for Wes Craven), and blah, blah, blah. Who else is falling asleep right now? Christ, the first *Nightmare* has been praised and analyzed to death! I don't want to write about it. You don't want to read about it. So let's just call it a draw and say that the first *Nightmare* is my favorite movie, but *Nightmare 2* is my favorite horror movie.

Now hold on a minute. Did this guy just say that *A Nightmare on Elm Street 2* is his favorite horror movie? The one with the exploding parakeet? You read that right. *Freddy's* motherfucking *Revenge* is my favorite horror movie. It's the sequel that hordes of Freddy fans loathe, seen as an awkward stepping stone to the far superior *Dream Warriors*. But not for me. During the height of my own Freddy mania, when I would cut out any *Nightmare* listings in the TV Guide and pin them to my cork board like a serial killer, it was *Freddy's Revenge* that I was most stoked to stay up late and watch. This was before I owned every *Nightmare* on VHS, DVD, and Blu-ray. And now that I own them all? *Freddy's Revenge* is the one I watch the most. The reason is simple: more than any other *Nightmare*, *Freddy's Revenge* captures very specific fears and anxieties that I experienced from middle school through high school. It's an odd duck, just like me.

Freddy's Revenge classically opens with a school bus ride from hell. Jesse, played by Mark Patton, is driven to a crumbling desert inferno by his new bus driver, Freddy Krueger. Terrified and cornered in the back of the bus, Jesse is almost slashed by Freddy until he wakes up screaming in his bed. At the end of the movie, after defeating the bogeyman and reclaiming his body, Jesse and Freddy take a final school bus safari straight into oblivion.

Let me get one thing straight: school bus drivers scare the shit out of me. I'll explain. When I was in first grade, my bus driver was a very scary and unpredictable old man. Some days he would let us be loud and and unruly, other days he would lose his mind at the slightest chatter from the back seats. Looking back on it now, this dude was obviously unstable. One day, the bus driver overheard me call a friend "butthead" on the ride home and that was some sort of a trigger for him. When we got to my stop, the bus driver followed me out of the bus, marched over to my mother, and screamed to her that I was a bad boy who used foul language and needed to be punished! He pointed a judgmental finger at me, jumped back in his bus, and drove away. Over dinner with my parents, I tearfully pleaded that I wasn't using curse words, and that the bus driver was a maniac. They seemed to believe me, but I'm still wary of school buses, and the *Freddy's Revenge* bus sequences still make me incredibly uneasy. The thought of that scary bus driver zooming past my stop and taking me somewhere to kill me? Brrrrr. It always enters my mind when watching *Freddy's Revenge*.

But it's not just a school bus thing. I've always found myself drawn to the character of Jesse and the performance of Mark Patton. Jesse is the awkward new kid in town, something I experienced when I moved to San Diego in the middle of fourth grade. Jesse dreaded P.E. because of an unsympathetic gym teacher; had a best friend who was somewhat antagonistic, and often made a fool of himself. Check. Check. Check. Of course, Patton's performance has been criticized for years, with many people mocking Jesse for screaming his lungs out a few times. But you know what? When I had nightmares of Freddy stalking me, I would scream the same way Jesse did - like my head was on fucking fire. How else are you gonna scream? It was so relatable and rare to have a male character actually respond to evil with raw terror. No tough guy posturing, no comic book heroics, just delirious helplessness. Yeah, I've felt that a few times.

But a *Nightmare* movie is only as good as its Freddy Krueger. For me personally, this is the scariest Freddy in the entire series. I know this is controversial. Many folks hate that Freddy only stalks Jesse in a quest to enter the real world, which basically annihilates all the rules set in place by Wes Craven. But this is exactly why I find Freddy so terrifying in this movie. Freddy isn't trying to kill Jesse. He's ripping Jesse to shreds, over and over, birthing himself into the real world to kill everybody close to Jesse. And Jesse feels this unimaginable pain over and over, without the release of death to ease his suffering. This, to me, is the greatest nightmare of all.

Freddy's Revenge also contains my favorite scene in the entire series: the pool party massacre. I know, Wes Craven said it's silly because some of the teenagers at the party look taller than Freddy Krueger. I don't care when I first saw it. That shit scared me to death and blew my mind at the same time. A universal truth that I always believed was safety in numbers. The bogeyman couldn't attack you in public with a bunch of people around. He would lure you away, get you alone, and strike when none of your friends could help you. But at a pool party? Holy shit! One minute these guys are cooking hot dogs and the next, Freddy is slashing their faces and gutting them! That freaked me out beyond all comprehension. This was a scene that would always haunt me, and one that I would revisit with more reflection as a high schooler during the era of Columbine.

Freddy's Revenge has been called the gayest slasher of all time. When I watched it as a kid, I didn't have a clue about the gay "subtext" that wallpapers the entire movie. But after the not-so-secret gay themes became apparent to me, my fondness for the movie only grew stronger. A box office hit like *Freddy's Revenge* unleashed on the public with subliminal and not-so-subliminal gayness? How amazingly punk rock is that? A lot of people are off-put by all the homoerotic imagery in the movie, but those people are intolerant scum. At its worst, it's campy as hell and I fucking love camp. At its best, it's slyly subversive and way ahead of its time. If you don't like *Freddy's Revenge* because it "doesn't work as a *Nightmare* movie," then that's totally fine. But if you don't like it because of "all that gay stuff," then you're the real nightmare and you need to wake up.

Along with reflecting my personal fears and anxieties, *Freddy's Revenge* is a maelstrom of anything goes rule-breaking that will always divide audiences. It's outside the box, it's camp, it's controversial. It's what I always strive to accomplish when writing and directing. It's also my favorite horror movie.

DEAD CALM
BY
BRANDON SLAGLE
Director
Crossbreed, House of Manson, The Dawn
Instagram: @BrandonSlagle

It's funny how we discover certain movies sometimes. These days, it's hard to really ignore anything that's being marketed on the gargantuan scale of films based on major IP's or even steaming exclusives on Netflix. I guess I'm getting older. Actually, strike the "guess" part. I know I am.

Even before nostalgia was en vogue, I always felt like the discovery – THE HUNT – that was associated with feature films decades ago was just as exciting, if not MORE exciting, than the end credit sequences in a Marvel movie teasing the exciting future to come.

I have fond memories of browsing mom-and-pop style video stores – both rental and sell-through – throughout various parts of the country growing up. One particular store whose name I cannot remember for the life of me used to hand me copies of the sales catalogs they ordered movies from once they were finished with each issue.

I'd browse these endlessly, enamored with the ad art for each movie as I thumbed through the pages. Some of these movies I would later see on the shelves in classic VHS form – some of them I'd forget and discover later in life for different reasons.

The funny thing about our tastes in art is that they change for various reasons as we mature. I guess that's why I mindlessly skimmed over the cover of a movie called *Dead Calm* when I was in junior high. The evocative shot of Nicole Kidman's face horizontally submerged in blood-red water may have been a bit too high brow for me at the time. Looking back at it now, it's still quite a bit more intense than the average modern movie poster.

A few short years later, I'd become a gigantic fan of industrial music. Bands such as KMFDM, Skinny Puppy, Frontline Assembly, Spahn Ranch, Godflesh – these were my gospel for years. For those of you who may not be familiar with these acts, they were the gateway drug to Nine Inch Nails, Gravity Kills, and Filter at one point in time.

I recall browsing the shelves of a video store when I was sixteen or so when I came upon a VHS copy of *Dead Calm*. I remembered it of course from seeing its poster in the trade magazines years earlier and - minus a random Tom Cruise interview where he claimed to have fallen in love with future ex-wife Nicole Kidman after watching it - I had forgotten this film existed.

I picked it up, looked over the synopsis and – being the future filmmaker I was becoming after getting a cheap VHS camcorder for Christmas – looked over the billing block on the back of the cover. I'd started paying attention to who did what job on each film.

One name jumped out at me – the composer - GRAEME REVELL. I knew this name for a couple of reasons: he had composed the Cajun-flavored score for John Woo's first American feature, *Hard Target*, and was the leader of an Australian industrial/noise act called SPK, which was rumored to be short for "Surgical Penis Klinik", though I don't believe that was ever confirmed.

That was it. SOLD. I rented *Dead Calm* that night. Good thing the clerks in video stores never thought to check ID to make sure I could rent R-rated movies, though I'm pretty sure they didn't care. I still remember my membership ID number at this fine establishment. It was 20951.

Needless to say, I used it quite a bit.

I was living with my paternal grandparents at the time after some close calls getting into some really bad trouble. Looking back, I completely understand my mother's decision. I don't remember if it was ever specifically stated, or I was just being respectful, but any time I rented an R-rated movie, I had to wait to watch it until everyone else had gone to sleep, just in case it happened to be a bit too much for my grandparents or any random visiting cousins. Anytime I didn't do this, it usually resulted in relatives less than half my age running in when Arnold Schwarzenegger proclaimed "Chill out, Dickwad," in *Terminator 2*. Thankfully, they rarely repeated any phrase I inadvertently helped them learn.

I popped in the VHS copy of *Dead Calm* that night with a bad frozen pizza and leaned back in my grandfather's nearby leather recliner. Right off the bat, the movie hits you in the chest with the death of a child. It isn't particularly stylized, sans slow motion. It isn't played for melodramatics. It just hits you. It hits you HARD.

I don't exactly remember what I expected. At my young age, I successfully survived numerous instances of Jason Voorhees popping up to deal with a protagonist before the end credits rolled, but this was something on an entirely new level I wasn't ready to deal with at the time.

The movie continued. There was something raw and nihilistic about the way it presented the loss of a child. It was unforgiving and didn't immediately rush into a soothing an-

ecdote the way that many films do now, instead opting to iso-
late the protagonists/parents portrayed by Sam Neill and the
aforementioned Kidman from the rest of the world on a boat
disguised as therapy.

I think this may have been one of the first times I really
paid attention to the theme and metaphor in a film. The characters sailing ALONE in the ocean wasn't meant to be taken
on face value, but as a metaphor for the isolation that tragedy
had gifted them. I may have related to it at the time for different reasons – I barely spent more than a semester in a school
before being forced to transfer to another one for years, so in a
way, I too felt like I'd been isolated on a boat in the middle of
the ocean.

Billy Zane (in a character type he didn't fully revisit as his
career went on) shines as the charming psychopath that drifts
(literally) into their lives. He claims to be the sole survivor of
a tragedy that befell a nearby boat, when in reality he was the
cause of this tragedy – bouncing from group to group.

I've known people like this. I could be reading too much
into this or making it too personal, but his character exempli-
fies the type of emotional vampires I was inherently drawn to
during my 20s. You befriend them. You want to help them. You
want the best for them. You've confided in them. Then they
turn that on you. It becomes their weapon. They drive people away from you, though not necessarily onto a nearby boat
full of hacked-up bodies as Billy Zane's character does – but it
might as well be the same thing.

Once again I may be making this too personal, but finding this type of emotional resonance to one's own experience
makes for the best works of art, at least as far as I'm concerned.
Paintings, movies, music...emotional resonance makes it all
better.

The music – that's right. That's what drew me back to this
film to begin with. Graeme Revell's score that combines elec-
tronics with ethnic percussion along with literal breathing and
gasping was unique at the time and as far as I'm aware, it's

unique to this day. Later Revell scores such as *The Crow* and its sequel were similarly experimental but nothing he has done since has approached the elegantly (and deliciously) primal yet coherent and structured as this score does. It really lives as its own character in the movie, working not as underscore but as the aural equivalent of sweat, saltwater, and a rapidly increasing heart rate.

Continuing my metaphorical interpretation of the film, Kidman is essentially trapped in a small space with an unrelenting antagonistic force. At the time, the living equivalent of that force for me would have been a natural shyness which made me a consistent target for bullies sporting endless supplies of testosterone and hometown pride. Any help I would have received was circling nearby but unreachable, just as Sam Neill's character is through most of *Dead Calm*'s running time (on a doomed vessel – eventually gasping for life itself). That could be just how I took it, but you can easily switch out each of these elements with any array of potentially negative influences in life. On one hand, life tempts you to give in to these outside forces, as Kidman's character does (in a ploy) to Zane's perceived desires towards her. On the other hand, often when we give in, we can come out stronger. Some call this desperation. Some call this survival mode.

Zane's character is dispatched twice, harpooned and sent into the abyss of the ocean at night, then later with a flare to the mouth. Just as trying to kill the seemingly unkillable villain is a familiar horror and thriller trope – ridding oneself of negative influences (such as the aforementioned emotional vampires) requires multiple attempts as well (though usually without the brutal force of harpoons and flares). Even once Zane or these influences is gone, there's no definite happy ending. We simply don't sail into the sunset. The future is unknown. Sometimes we make the same mistakes, sometimes we don't. It's definitely grim when so many films of today are left open for a sequel, not that anything's wrong with that.

As the decades went on, *Dead Calm* has shown to have incredible staying power with me. Any time I've revisited it over the years, it carries the same grim, visceral impact it did the first time. Maybe it's the nostalgia goggles, but it literally never loses the impact.

As I grew into a musician in my early to mid-20s, and later into an actor-turned-filmmaker as I got older, the same themes that resonated in this film with me have managed to pop up here and there. Though I seem to have a knack for popcorn movie fare and people running around with machine guns, that sense of nihilism and character despair, which some may call downbeat, often manages to come through whether in writing, pre-production, actual production, or post-production. Sometimes it works well, and sometimes it's not quite right for the piece and gets removed. Sometimes the owner (sales company or distributor) of the film adds conflicting tonal elements for sales purposes – which could be an entire essay of its own.

Dead Calm's influences definitely persist. Beyond even popping up in my own works, I look forward to revisiting it in my '60s, '70s, and '80s (on Hulu or however people watch movies then), to experience it the same way I did when I was a punk teenager staying up late to watch R-rated movies.

POLTERGEIST (1982)
BY
MEREDITH BORDERS

Freelance Writer/Managing Editor
Fangoria
Twitter/Instagram: @Xymarla

While it's fair to say that my parents didn't let me watch much horror growing up, the truth is that I wasn't allowed to watch much of anything. We're a family of readers, and television and film were never prioritized in my household. Most of our VHSes were straight-to-video Christian family films. We rarely went to the cinema, and I lived in a small town whose video store didn't offer much in the way of broadening my cinematic horizons.

But I knew I loved horror, even before I knew what that meant.

I loved being scared. I'd scare myself sometimes on purpose, crafting elaborately dark scenarios in my mind about what was in the shadowy corner, or under the bed. I was drawn to the spooky section of the library or school book fair, to the

Blockbuster cover art of films I knew my parents would never let me take home. I caught glimpses of A *Nightmare on Elm Street* at my much older cousin's house and thought, "Yes. This is what I want."

Poltergeist was the first horror movie I watched in its entirety. It played on TV after my parents and big sister had gone to bed, and I remember with such clarity the thrill of doing two things I wasn't supposed to be doing: eating peanut butter straight out of the jar while licking the spoon clean and then sticking it right back in for more, and watching a scary movie.

Poltergeist is a perfect gateway movie for a budding horror lover. So much of the film is built on wholesome and believable family dynamics. The Freelings felt familiar, felt real. I cared about them instantly – about Steve's football parties and Robbie's anxieties, about Carol Anne's funeral for her pet bird Tweety, and the way Diane got the giggles. (I didn't grasp why the grownups were quite so jolly in that scene, but I dug it, anyway.) And while almost all horror movies focus on terrified teenagers or adults, *Poltergeist* is about what I was when I saw it: a little girl.

Heather O'Rourke gives such a gifted performance as Carol Anne Freeling. She doesn't have that hard-edged, self-conscious presentation of a child actor used to commercials and laugh tracks. She's soft and quirky and genuine. When she takes a half-chewed Twizzler out of her mouth and puts it in Tweety's shoebox murmuring, "For when he's hungry," my heart still clenches. The tragedy that O'Rourke's talent didn't survive the *Poltergeist* franchise makes her first performance all the more precious. As an adult, I mourn that sweet little girl who never made it to her teens. As a kid, all I knew was that I liked Carol Anne, I related to her, and she was in danger.

Of course, a third of the way through the film, Carol Anne disappears for much of *Poltergeist's* screen time, but by the time she's sucked into that unfathomable portal in her bedroom closet, I was already hooked. It didn't hurt that the set piece that ends with her disappearance is, to this day, one of the most breathtakingly bonkers scenes in any horror movie before or since. The energetic spirits inhabiting the Freelings' home start small, but not slow. After a pleasant evening of kitchen chairs sliding autonomously across the floor, delighting Diane and Carol Anne, suddenly the sky opens up, a tree tries to eat poor Robbie, the kids' bedroom turns upside down and Carol Anne's closet transforms into a vast maw hungry for child. It all happens in minutes, and when it's over, Carol Anne has vanished, the Freelings are forever changed, and I was a horror fan for life.

Somehow, *Poltergeist* only gets cooler from there. It's a cleverly paced and plotted story: it spends a little time establishing the Freelings as a family we love and want to keep safe. The night Carol Anne is sucked into the world behind the television grabs our attention, and the rest of the film is balanced between increasingly horrific scares with all-timer FX (I'm still in love with the scene where Marty peels off his face in front of the bathroom mirror, an image that burrowed itself into my neural pathways that night and never left), and moments of compelling emotional pathos that remind us that the Freelings are a real family suffering a terrifying loss. All the latex and red-dyed corn syrup may make for a good time, but our hearts are always breaking for Steve and Diane; for Robbie and Dana. We have that in common with Tangina Barrons, the spiritual medium brought in to bring Carol Anne back from the other side. Zelda Rubinstein plays Tangina with utter empathy and compassion, and the deep feeling she has for the Freelings' plight only intensifies our own.

Poltergeist is scary for a lot of reasons – because of the monster in the closet, the corpses in the pool, the steak crawling across the kitchen counter, because of the unequivocal appetite of this otherwise unremarkable suburban home, a home that looked like a lot of houses in 1982. A home that looked like my house.

But it's scariest because it's a movie that asks – that insists – that we give a damn about its characters. I did, as an eight-year-old kid with a mouth full of peanut butter and a heart thrilling at my new secret passion. I cared about that family and I was afraid for them, and my fear felt right and good and dangerous and fun. I've chased that feeling ever since, but few films in my life have ever delivered it as elegantly as *Poltergeist*.

NIGHT OF THE LIVING DEAD
(1968)
BY
CHRIS GORE

Author/Filmmaker/Magazine Founder/Host
*Film Threat, Film Threat Podcast, Attack of the Show,
Chris Gore's Ultimate Film Festival Survival Guide*
Facebook: @ILikeChrisGore Twitter: @ThatChrisGore
ThatChrisGore.com

Zombies. Ghouls. The living dead. The 1968 black and white version of George Romero's *Night of the Living Dead* is not only my all-time favorite horror film, it is an independent movie that created a genre and changed the industry. Before I delve into my own history with this horror milestone and the profound impact it had on my life, it's important to point out why it remains one of the most terrifying films of all time. A movie that inspired sequels and remakes, novels, video games, toys, comic books, television series and nightmares. A classic that has stood the test of time with its influence continuing to echo more than 50 years later.

Exactly why is *Night of the Living Dead* still so terrifying? The zombies or "ghouls" as they are referred to in the original, are rotting, disfigured, bloody, and scarred humans. These are not monsters from a horror flick in the traditional sense like some reptilian sea creature or fanged vampire, or an antennaed-alien from another world. No, the ghouls in George Romero's films, sometimes referred to as the "Romeroverse," are reanimated people. They are us. Our mothers, fathers, brothers and sisters, children, friends and neighbors. The people that are alive and well must deal with unimaginable trauma as they are forced to battle former loved ones with a taste for flesh. This horrific thought has haunted me from the very first time I watched *Night of the Living Dead* as a single-digit-aged boy in suburban Michigan.

It should be no surprise to you that I was a pretty weird kid, born with an obsession for comic books and monster movies. I was a voracious reader and watcher of films, and as an indoor kid, I put together my share of Aurora model kits. My mom tells me that I learned to read at a very young age, mainly so that I could scan the TV listings to find out what science fiction and monster movies were playing that week. It was in the *TV Guide* that I noticed the title *Night of the Living Dead*. The movie would play on a Saturday night on channel 50 in Detroit on *The Ghoul Show*. I worshipped the Ghoul, which featured horror host and comedic genius Ron Sweed. The Ghoul put on little comedy bits that played between the movies, like using firecrackers to blow up model kits, Super 8 shorts made by fans, a toy character he tortured called Froggy, and generally a juvenile sense of humor often accompanied by the sound of farts. I loved it. But even the comedic wraparounds provided by the Ghoul did not shield me from the horrific thoughts after seeing *Dead* for the first time. I recall having trouble sleeping as I imagined my friends and family turning on me, as one by one, they turned into ghouls. There is something primal in our lizard brains that makes the simple act of "being chased while trying to avoid being eaten" so frightening.

In addition, there was that ending. This was the first time I had ever seen a movie that did not end well. There was no "happy ending." Nobody survives. Witnessing the hero Ben, played with cold cool by Duane Jones, actually live to see the light of day, only to be mistaken for a ghoul and tragically killed, meant that the good guys don't always win. When Ben meets his end, there's no one left to tell his heroic tale. He's burned with the rest of the dead over graphic photos and a haunting musical score. That first viewing of *Night of the Living Dead* left me scarred for life. Yes, I slept with the light on.

I'd seen my share of monster movies on weekly horror shows like *Creature Feature* and *Sir Graves Ghastly*, but nothing affected me quite the same as *Night of the Living Dead*. Thoughts of zombies being the cause of humanity's undoing as society collapsed became an obsession for me. My friends and I even invented our own playground game in which a person tagged then became a zombie and sought to turn others into zombies with the goal of being the last surviving human. The entire neighborhood was the setting, and as a kid, the only thing scarier than the film was playing this game in the black of night.

Seeing *Night of the Living Dead* on television was an experience that I wished to have without the disruption of commercials or even my hero the Ghoul. I was on a mission to see *Dead* uncut. So, with the money saved from delivering newspapers, I got a Super 8 film projector from Thomas Film Classics and proceeded to build a makeshift movie theater in my home. (It was the '70s and this was before VHS players became commonplace.)

I convinced my mom to allow me to use our laundry chute as a projection booth. I was small enough to crawl into this tiny space and cut out a hole in the drywall into the next room. I carefully placed the projector onto a chair to screen movies in my basement and I even ran speaker wire into the makeshift theater, so only the sound of the film could be heard. My friends were so impressed as the clacking of the projector was silenced when I screened Buster Keaton and Laurel and Hardy classics. I imagine this was the closest thing to a home theater one could have back in the day.

All of this was in preparation to watch the unedited version of *Night of the Living Dead* in Super 8. It was rare that entire features were even available for purchase. This was the wild west of home entertainment days, but I was dying to see *Dead* uncut. Over the summer, I saved money from my allowance, mowing lawns and delivering newspapers for what seemed like an eternity. And the day finally came when I had enough cash, I bought the 1968 George Romero classic on Super 8, a sound print which came on two giant reels. I still remember the smell of the film, yes, it was actual film and you could hold it up to the light to see those glorious images on individual frames.

I soon realized that all the neighborhood kids and their parents could not fit into my makeshift basement theater, so we ended up screening the film outdoors by projecting onto the side of the garage in my backyard. Somehow, I was able to turn my ingenuity and geekiness into a way to become popular with this neighborhood event. And that popularity increased immensely when I served bowls of popcorn while we watched the uncut version which revealed brief shots of nudity to the delight of all the kids! Seeing the look of fear on everyone's face as the credits rolled made it all worth it.

George Romero's vision continued with the release of *Dawn of the Dead* and *Day of the Dead*, both of which I saw on opening day in a theater. *Dawn* was yet another milestone with that shocking shot of the exploding head in the opening sequence. The final mall scenes were terrifying and no character, no matter how likable, was safe in *Dawn*. While *Day of the Dead* didn't live up to my expectations, I just remember loving good ol' Bub. I thought the trilogy was the end, and that we'd never see Romero zombies on screen again. But in 1989, I learned that they were going to produce a remake of *Night of the Living Dead* directed by master of gore effects Tom Savini. Through *Film Threat*, I had become friends with JJ Hommel, a filmmaker who told me that I could be a zombie in the remake. I just had to get to the set in Pittsburgh fast. Nothing was going to stop me.

I drove to Pittsburgh from Detroit stopping only for bathroom breaks, arriving late to the farmhouse where they were shooting. I was never more star struck than when I met George Romero, all smiles, standing proudly on set. I crashed on the couch of the make-up effects team of John Vulich and Everett Burrell. I was kind of their mascot for the shoot as they taught me about old school make-up effects. Before I could appear on camera, I had to attend zombie school with other extras where I would learn how to walk, how to follow instructions from the assistant director, and learn what "back to one" meant on a film set.

At that point in my career, I had visited very few film sets, but I knew talent was treated differently. For the *Dead* remake, things were different -- no elitism or big egos -- this was independent filmmaking in its purest form, with everyone equal and putting forth their best efforts to honor the 1968 original. I hung out with the cast which quickly became a family -- Tony Todd, Patricia Tallman, Tom Towles, and William Butler, who remains a friend to this day. The production crew, effects team, the extras, the lead actors, all of us came together because our lives were changed by the original film. Among the dead extras were longtime friend Dennis Daniel and legendary cartoonist Gahan Wilson, all of us bound by our love of Romero and zombies. Every person on the film was there because they were moved by the black and white original. The production felt less like a film set and more like going to camp with everyone telling personal stories about the first time they saw *Night of the Living Dead* during those long night shoots.

For my scenes, I stood with a group of other zombies, and slowly lumbered down a hill before hearing "cut" and then being told to "go back to one." When the long nights ended, I was dead tired but ready to do it all again. My experience ended in a way I could never have imagined -- being directed by Savini himself in a key scene. I played a featured zombie as I dragged the charred remains of the character of Tom (actually a dummy of the character played by William Butler) out of the burned-out truck. I then had to dive in to devour what was a steaming stew of guts made from cold, barbecued chicken. I don't even recall if I ever got paid, but I did receive a signed certificate from Tom Savini himself declaring that I appeared as a zombie in *Night of the Living Dead*. I still have the certificate to this day.)

Whatever you think of the *Dead* sequels or remakes, the original *Night of the Living Dead* has left an indelible mark on film history. Whether he meant to or not, George Romero created the zombie movie genre. There's no doubt that the *Dead* films are a franchise, with one very important difference. While Romero clearly created the rules followed by all zombie fiction (shoot them in the head) he never copyrighted those rules to prevent other creatives from playing in his universe. And while other films like *Return of the Living Dead* altered the rules somewhat, and *The Walking Dead* TV series has become, well, like a zombie that just will not die. Every zombie film, novel, comic book, video game and TV show owes a tremendous debt to Mr. George Romero. Thank you George for keeping us up late at night...with the light on.

CARRIE (1976)
BY
GREGORY BLAIR

Actor, Writer, Director
*Garden Party Massacre, Deadly Revisions, Fang
The Ritual, Little Shivers*
GregoryBlair.info
Twitter/Facebook/Instagram: @TheGregoryBlair

Are you kidding me!?!
What is this: *Sophie's Choice*…times ten?!?

That is always my first thought when someone asks me to name my favorite horror movie. The genre is so disparate, choosing seems impossible. Subject matter varies from slashers to monster movies, psychological horror, tales of the paranormal, and so on; visual styles range from lyrical and beautiful to visceral and repulsive; sensibilities range from moody and creepy to assaultive and shocking. Even within the subgenres, there can be very different, but equally brilliant animals. Comparing and rating them seems like cruel and unusual punishment. To ask me to pick only one as some sort of "best" is truly the definition of horror!

So, with a proverbial gun to my head, I'm going to hoist one above the others; not because it's necessarily "better than," but because it stands out to me as one that represents the widest range of what the genre is (or can be) about. And, I'll do my best to explain why—before there is any bloodletting...

It may be because I first saw the film in my teenage years—when emotions are higher, and things often have more impact. That, and the fact that it was about a teenager and the horrors of high school, made the film resonate so much for me, but Brian De Palma's *Carrie* surprised me on so many levels that, despite its age, remains high on my list. In my mind, that is the definition of a classic: it manages to transcend the era of its creation. *Carrie* offers many ingredients that made it (and continue to make it) stand out—its narrative choices, stylistic signatures, and powerhouse casting are three that make it easy to choose when forced to pick a "best".

First, the narrative. King's novel certainly laid the groundwork for the *Cinderella* story gone horribly wrong, but De Palma's film (thanks to the Lawrence D. Cohen screenplay) brings so much unexpected heart and humor to the tale that, had Carrie not possessed supernatural powers, the story still could have worked as a realistic modern tragedy. But the powers exist and De Palma uses them as an increasingly creepy element while we watch Carrie's evolution in wielding them. The film gets very scary, but what sucks you in is the powerless horror that Carrie suffers from the bullies at school and at home; her religious kook mother, Margaret White, proving the worst bully, and the love/hate dynamic between her as the abuser and Carrie as the victim is heartbreaking to watch. We have all been victims of cruelty at some time in our lives and so we relate to Carrie and root for her to overcome her detractors—even though we fear how she may do it and what damage may result. In short, the story speaks to the ugliness of humanity: scapegoating and bullying, demonizing biology, religious fanaticism, child abuse and more. Perhaps if society were not so monstrous, people like Carrie would be welcomed, loved and nurtured to become heroes instead of villains. This is the evocative nature of great storytelling and something that always makes a film more exciting and meaningful.

Then there are De Palma's signature stylistic touches that cinematically augment the emotions and themes of the piece - too many for one essay, but here are some of my favorites. First, the spinning dance shot. De Palma put the actors on a platform that spun in one direction and the camera circled them in the other…faster and faster. The effect perfectly makes the audience as dizzy as Carrie must be feeling in that moment. Just like that conflated love/hate sensibility, the characters' smiles make you feel the joy they are feeling in that moment, but you know the horrible thing that's about to happen, so the joy is mixed with anxiety for the horror to come—as well as a deep empathy and sadness for poor Carrie who has no idea it's nigh. The first time I saw this moment, I was moved to tears. Another brilliant choice is when Carrie is blood-drenched on stage and De Palma uses a kaleidoscope effect to turn nasty Norma's hideous laughter into a room full of people laughing; letting us know that everyone is NOT laughing at Carrie, but that she is just seeing it that way. And the cause? Back to the number one bully: mother. Over this kaleidoscope effect we hear Mrs. White's voice repeating in an echo "They're all going to laugh at you!" So, this woman's brow-beating negativity manifests into Carrie imagining that everyone is laughing at her; that everyone has betrayed her; that they all deserve to be punished—punishment being another lesson learned from mother. The takeaway being that Carrie's revenge is largely a result of everything she learned from her mother—the true monster of the movie. This kind of filmmaking—where the artistic elements augment the themes through calibrated visuals and sounds—makes movies more thrilling. I try to emulate that in a variety of ways in my own films and, in *Deadly Revisions*, I slip in winks to some of my favorite directors, including a classic DePalma nod.

Finally, there's the stellar performances of the cast all around. Both Sissy Spacek (Carrie) and Piper Laurie (Margaret White) were nominated for Oscars—something we all know rarely happens for a horror film. Depending on the moment in the film, Sissy shows us—with a single look—Carrie's vulnerability, her love, her frustration and ultimately, her rage. Laurie is the living litmus test to how far an actor can go in portraying the psychopath that might live next door…or under our own roof. The supporting cast (Amy Irving, Betty Buckley, William Katt, Nancy Allen, P. J. Soles and John Travolta) all bring their A-game to Cohen's well-defined characters, making them very real and effective. Not every horror film boasts such perfection and talent in those who bring its characters to vivid, memorable life, but *Carrie* delivers that with a bang.

So…back to the proverbial gun and my version of *Sophie's Choice*. To be clear: when it comes to art, subjectivity is fair game. One's choice is inarguably correct for them, whether they can back it up or not. That said, while I'd agonize over all the children I'd be setting aside to pick "the one," should anyone dare to question my decision in choosing *Carrie*, I'd take comfort in knowing that I'm armed with manifold reasons why and can wield them like superpowers at a prom from hell.

PHANTASM
BY
NATASHA PASCETTA

Writer/Director/Producer/Director of Digital Production
Fangoria, Road Trash, Class of Podcast
Instagram: @NatashaPascetta
Apple Podcasts: *Class Of*

S tarting high school is one of the scariest things you can experience. As an awkward fourteen-year-old, I was terrified about my eventual fate as a high schooler. I can very clearly remember the night before the first day of ninth grade. I was a mess. That night, I also made a decision that would go on to affect my life in ways I could never have known.

I rented *Phantasm* from Wow Video.

I honestly had no idea what the movie was about. I just knew I liked the sound of the title and I needed a movie to distract my nervous mind from the impending reality that I was about to start high school. So I popped in the tape and was immediately taken by the characters, especially Mike.

Mike's fearlessness in the brief scene where he and the Tall

Man engage in a choreographed western-style dance inside Morningside Mortuary before Mike flees astounded me. This kid had balls.

In a way, I saw the movie as an allegory for me entering ninth grade. If Mike could take on the Tall Man, his army of undead dwarves and flying metal spheres, surely I could take on Gloucester Catholic High School.

The next morning, I stepped onto the school bus and felt like I had passed through the interdimensional portal. I was scared. But then I saw something that gave me some coincidental reassurance. We passed a fleet of ice cream trucks. I could hear Reg in my head say, "We lay that sucker out flat and drive a stake right through his Goddamn heart!"

I smiled to myself and knew I could handle anything ninth grade threw my way.

Just as *Phantasm* helped me get over my fear of high school, it has also helped me understand and accept a much deeper fear: death.

I had the opportunity to interview Don Coscarelli on my podcast and he recounted how he vividly remembers the genesis of *Phantasm*. He was seven years old, lying in bed, when it suddenly dawned on him that he was going to die. That his parents were going to die. Death was not just inevitable, it was a promise. Pretty deep for a seven year old!

I think I find this weird comfort and acceptance in the Tall Man as a harbinger of death. Just like Don, I am not in denial that I'm going to expire—but I hope something as bizarre and strange as the Tall Man and his minions are on the other side. Because, well, that's a more exciting option than nothing.

It wasn't until years later that I came to truly understand and appreciate the labor of love Don Coscarelli and his team put into *Phantasm*. The movie serves as a bright beacon of independent filmmaking. Don literally willed this movie and its characters into existence and, now, they will live on forever in the hearts and minds of fans. As a fledgling filmmaker myself, I look to the production of *Phantasm* for constant inspiration and motivation.

It's no coincidence that I chose to prominently feature a cemetery and a main character with an obsession for burying things in my first short film, *Road Trash.*

I love *Phantasm* so much, that for its 40th anniversary in 2019, I helped organize a "hearse stuffing" contest sponsored by *Fangoria* at the Alamo Drafthouse as a homage to the Avco Embassy publicity stunt that was used to promote the original release of *Phantasm* in 1979. We fit 30 (live!) fans into a hearse, beating the previous record of 27! There were many people at the event that had never seen the movie before and I felt a great deal of joy being able to introduce *Phantasm* to new fans. It was a memory that I will cherish forever.

The mystique of Morningside Mortuary continues to capture my imagination, the hard work and passion that Don Coscarelli put into the movie continues to inspire me and, to this day, I try to keep Mike's fortitude within my heart whenever I feel I need a shot of confidence.

INVASION OF
THE BODY SNATCHERS
(1978)
BY
ETHAN REIFF

Screenwriter/Showrunner/Executive Producer
*Tales from the Crypt Presents: Demon Knight,
Brimstone, Bulletproof Monk, Sleeper Cell,
Kung Fu Panda, Eleventh Hour*

"You will be born again into an untroubled world,
free from anxiety, fear, hate."

I first heard those words on Christmas Eve 1978, spoken by a heinous yet banal villain in *Invasion of the Body Snatchers.* I was thirteen at the time and lived in Brooklyn, New York with my mom, dad, and ten-year-old younger brother. In 1978, almost all of New York City was filthy and dangerous. The best cinematic representation I know of is *Taxi Driver,* shot in Manhattan in 1976. Some say its portrayal of the city is stylized and extreme, but I find it painstakingly accurate. If you asked back then, I would have said something along the lines of: "Horror movies are bullshit. If you really want to be scared, try living in New York."

Please bear with me. Before getting deeper into 1978's *Body Snatchers*, I have to tell you a little more about my family. At home, our mom took both the lead and supporting roles as a parent. She was and remains a highly energized creative force of nature. If not for her influence, I doubt my brother (who is a successful TV showrunner) or myself would have chosen and succeeded at our creative careers. Our dad, who passed away in December 2013, just under thirty-five years to the day since we watched *Invasion of the Body Snatchers*, was a good man. He was a dependable provider, and a good role model in some ways. Foremost among these was modelling behavior that taught us the importance of work. He was sixteen years older than our mom, had grown up during the Great Depression, served in the U.S. Army in India and the Pacific Islands during World War Two. He worked for a year as a chicken farmer on a kibbutz in Israel, learned to despise chickens, and left. He was incredibly handy and could drive any car, truck or motorcycle. He could also sail any small craft, thanks to having worked at a ship's supply store in Manhattan's South Street Seaport as a kid. After returning from Israel, he'd worked at a variety of building trades, and by 1978, he was the manager of the largest lumber yard in the Bronx. But with all that knowledge and experience, he never taught my brother or me how to drive, sail, change a tire, or hammer a nail. We knew he loved *Sherlock Holmes* stories, Frank Herbert's *Dune* books, and -- somewhat surprisingly for a Jewish guy from the Bronx -- bagpipe music. He'd heard it while stationed in India, which at the time was still part of the British Empire. We knew he loved us, but during the entire course of our childhoods, there were only a few moments when he expressed it. This is the story of how I discovered my favorite horror movie, and also the story of one of those moments.

It starts on Christmas Eve 1978 with an old Jewish American tradition: going to the movies. For some reason that year, our family didn't go to one of the few theaters still in business within easy reach of our neighborhood. Instead, we drove all the way across Brooklyn to King's Plaza -- the only enclosed mall in New York City; a little slice of suburbia that had been inexplicably parachute-dropped into the urban world of King's County. So things were kind of weird from the start that night. The movie was *Invasion of the Body Snatchers*. Not the 1956 B&W sci-fi/horror classic directed by Don Siegel from a screenplay by Daniel Mainwaring, based on the novel *The Body Snatchers* by Jack Finney (which I had not yet seen), but the remake directed by Philip Kaufman from a screenplay by W. D. Richter, based on the same Jack Finney novel. Some will prefer to label this version of *Body Snatchers* as science fiction rather than horror. Fair enough. I plead guilty to this being a genre-bending essay. Still, the thirteen-year-old me was POSITIVE it was a horror movie -- because it scared the living shit out of me. But its ultimate fright was served up after the credits rolled, courtesy of my dad. It was one of those few moments when he went out of his way to connect with my brother and me. It was an exercise in sheer terror, but it also made for an indelibly happy memory, which is why I share it with you now.

The movie starts on another planet. Yes, it is an "alien" planet, but not in the typical sci-fi form thirteen-year-old me was used to. There is nothing on this planet but an otherworldly version of nature. No spaceships, no Martians, no technology of any kind. Just a creepy cross between cobwebs and protoplasm. A viscous, mucusy, Vile Gunk. As it bubbles along the surface, it's accompanied by disturbing primordial murmurs, simultaneously repellent and intriguing sounds that might bring to mind the chirp of baby chicks from hell, accompanied by music that shifts back-and-forth from taut thriller to pastoral harmony without feeling clunky or forced.

The cutting-edge score was composed by jazz piano master Denny Zeitlin, who was already famous in musical circles for having helped pioneer the use of electronic keyboards and synthesizers alongside acoustic instruments in the world of jazz, while simultaneously working as a clinical professor of psychiatry.

Zeitlin is only one of a long list of incredibly talented artists and craftspeople recruited by Director Philip Kaufman to help make this version of *Invasion of the Body Snatchers* into what has been called the greatest remake ever made. Two others include: Director of Photography Michael Chapman, whose exceptional cinematography mixes detached documentary observation with moody, foreboding style (one of the most accomplished DPs in history, Chapman shot multiple films for Kaufman, and also Martin Scorsese, including *Taxi Driver*), and Production Designer Charles Rosen, whose version of San Francisco looks and feels incredibly real (in a completely different way from how he had helped make Martin Scorcese's New York feel real in *Taxi Driver*), which in turn makes the horrors that occur there more scary.

Back on the alien planet, the Vile Gunk floats off into space. It glides through the solar system like plankton in the ocean, or sperm through a uterus, until -- at about a minute-and-a-half of running time -- its POV reveals the blue and white marble of Earth. Only ninety-seconds in and not a word of dialogue, but I already knew this was not going to end well. The dramatic tension ratcheted up to maximum and my thirteen-year-old mind was racing: what is that stuff...and what will it do to us?!

The Vile Gunk POV descends through thick cloud cover and lands in the city of San Francisco. Not my hometown of NYC, but not all that different. It's raining, and it's deposited onto trees and bushes in a park, where it clings, spreads, and grows into pods, which then sprout pretty pink flowers. Whatever this stuff is, it grows at warp speed!

An attractive woman picks one of the flowers and takes it home. Along the way she passes a class of elementary school students whose teacher unknowingly instructs them: "Pick the beautiful flowers. Don't they smell nice!" Those kids were younger than me -- hell, they were younger than my ten-year-old little brother! To punctuate the threat, there's an eerie-looking priest on a nearby swing, watching the kids through deadpan eyes as he goes up and down...up and down.

The attractive woman is Elizabeth Driscoll. As played by Brooke Adams (*Days of Heaven* and *Dead Zone*), she projects an appealing combination of intelligent confidence and sweet vulnerability. She takes the flower back to her house and tries to tell her live-in boyfriend Geoffrey Howell about it (or maybe he's her husband? Their relationship, like those of virtually all the other characters, defy absolute clarity), but he's too busy watching playoff basketball. She puts the pretty flower in a vase and sets it on a nightstand near their bed. He tries to have sex with her, but she'd rather read. She's searching for that flower in a botany manual. Geoffrey puts on his c.1978 high tech headphones and goes back to watching the game. You get the impression they share living space and not much else.

CUT TO a peep-hole fish-eye lens view of Health Inspector Dr. Matthew Bennell. He gains entry to an expensive French restaurant and confronts the pompous owner with a rat turd from one of his kitchen pots. The owner claims it's a caper. Bennell uses his extra-long health department tweezers to hold it up in front of the owner's face and says: "If it's a caper ...eat it." He wins the debate and writes the place up for permit revocation. As played by the oddball yet charismatic Donald Sutherland, we know from the start that Matthew Bennell is a man of integrity. He may be a cog in a machine, but we're happy he's there. In the big city, someone has to make sure the rules are being followed, at least the ones that protect us from things like rat turds in over-priced gourmet cuisine. Some angry employees from the restaurant bust the window of Matthew's car and silently dare him to do something about it. But he keeps his composure and drives home through streets filled with police sirens and news reports about power failures. At age thirteen, I'd never been to San Francisco, but after this scene, it was a place I recognized, a place where society/civilization seemed poised on the quiet verge of collapse, same as my hometown. We learn Matthew and Elizabeth are Health Department colleagues. He collects samples in the field, she tests them in her lab. They're educated and sophisticated, but seem to share a sincere dedication to their jobs as civil servants. And they seem to like each other.

The next morning Elizabeth notices Geoffrey is even more disengaged than usual. Disturbingly so. He's up super early to deposit trash in a garbage truck that's waiting for him at the curb. At the lab, Elizabeth tells Matthew about Geoffrey's odd behavior. She's worried he's somehow become a different person.

Elizabeth and Matthew form the central relationship of the movie. Are they friends or colleagues, or unrequited lovers? It's pretty clear that Matthew has been pining away for Elizabeth since long before we meet them. But does Elizabeth feel the same? We don't yet know her true feelings towards Matthew, except that she trusts him enough to confide her fears about the man she lives with.

Matthew's unsure what to do. Elizabeth's boyfriend Geoffrey is better looking than him, has a better career, more money, and owns his own house. There could be a serious up-side for Matthew if Elizabeth decides to act on her arguably crazy conspiracy theory and break up with Geoffrey. It could finally have a chance with the woman he loves. But despite his long curly hair and porn-star mustache, Matthew Bennell has an old-school sense of right and wrong. So instead of making a move on Elizabeth in her moment of vulnerability, he introduces her to another friend: noted psychiatrist and self-help guru Dr. David Kibner.

Kibner is played by Leonard Nimoy, already famous to thirteen-year-old me as Mr. Spock from the original (sole legitimate) *Star Trek*. Like Spock, Kibner is a contradiction, a source of solace and wisdom, but also arrogant and off-putting. He wears a strange leather half-glove that may qualify as the most pretentious affectation wardrobe detail in movie history. What the hell is it for? Is it required by Starfleet, or does he wear it to hide an ugly scar? In hindsight it must be meant to serve as a visual clue, warning us not to trust Dr. Kibner's sage advice, because he is hiding something, and it's not just the back of his hand.

Elizabeth tells Kibner her fear that Geoffrey has somehow been changed into a completely different person, living a secret life as part of a conspiracy. Kibner listens, then tells her it's much more likely she's concocting ways to convince herself that Geoffrey is "different," so she'll have an excuse to end their relationship. A relationship which the two of them have built with time and effort, which has true value, and which he hopes she will consider trying to maintain. Elizabeth says she'll think about it. Kibner tells Matthew it's like there's a "hallucinatory flu" going around. Recently he's heard the exact same story from tons of people. Luckily, they all get over it in a day or two. Matthew asks if the Health Department should get involved, but everyone knows mental illness isn't contagious, so Kibner just laughs and tells Matthew he should take Elizabeth home to her boyfriend.

The story proceeds down a dark path of increasing paranoia and shrinking escape routes for our human heroes. A few select highlights: Matthew visits the dry cleaner to drop off dirty laundry. The Chinese laundry woman is needlessly stern and confrontational. When she takes his shirts to the back, her husband waves Matthew over to ask for help, and confides: "That not my wife!" Matthew asks if she's sick, but the husband says no, she's just "wrong;" shots of pedestrians walking crowded sidewalks and crossing crowded intersections, but always framed low, so it's just masses of nondescript feet, legs, and lower mid-sections, making the crowd of people seem more like a swarm of bees or school of fish; a maintenance man working one of those electric floor cleaners while he watches Matthew, ever the civil servant, work the phones in an effort to get help through government channels. In the end this just makes it easier for the Pods to keep track of Matthew and his friends.

There are two more of these: Jack Bellicec is a close friend of Matthew. He's a struggling writer who wears a trench coat over an army surplus jacket. We meet him at another author's book party, for whom he makes no effort to hide his contempt and jealousy. The sullen and self-absorbed Jack is played by an impossibly young Jeff Goldblum.

The last of the four leads is Jack's wife, Nancy Bellicec, played by Veronica Cartwright (who one year later in 1979 would be stalked aboard the *USCSS Nostromo* by a different kind of *Alien*). Nancy is a vibrant and passionate hard worker who supports her husband's creative endeavors. Together they own and operate a combined mud bath and massage parlor. Jack and Nancy's characters should be familiar to veterans of the low-budget filmmaking wars and aspiring creative types in general. Together they've carved out a niche where they can earn a living while simultaneously allowing Jack to pursue his literary dreams. Jack hasn't made the best-seller list and the mud baths aren't making them rich, but at least they have each other.

In fact, while Jack and Nancy are the most bohemian, fringe characters in the movie, they are also the only ones with a full-time, fully-functional relationship. It's true, Nancy has to serve as hostess for obese older male customers who enjoy their naked mud baths and massages, but nothing inappropriate is going on -- until the Pods show up at the massage parlor and things get really freaky.

This is how it works: the pretty flowers from space make you drowsy. You fall asleep and their wispy tendrils reach out and latch onto your flesh. The pod grows to XXXL size. The petals of its flower spread open like a pregnant woman's legs and spew out a pulsing proto-human, resembling a giant fetus, complete with fine hair and wax covering. It's hard to believe but the sound effects that accompany this process are as disturbing as the visuals. In an hour the giant fetus forms into a perfect POD PERSON copy of YOU -- at which point the original human version crumples into a gray husk. That's what the garbage trucks have been collecting across the city since that first morning at Geoffrey's house: the remains of real humans! At first it's hard for our four heroes to accept that otherworldly flowers are a serious threat, responsible for all the creepy conspiratorial shit that's been going on. But with a subversive glint in her eyes, Nancy asks the others: "Why not a space flower? Why do we always expect metal ships?"

In one of the movie's most twisted scenes, Matthew comes face to face with his own gestating Pod Person, lying at his feet. He pauses for a momentary existential crisis before bashing his own skull in with a garden hoe. And that's when we hear it. The SCREECH. It's the sound of the hive. The sound all the other Pod People make when something's wrong. Case in point, one almost fully-baked member of their collective organism being hacked to pieces. It's a cry of pain and mourning, but also an alarm. Now, all of Pod City knows there are a few O.G. humans still in need of body snatching. This, and all the other incredible special sound effects were created by Ben Burtt (who also created the sounds for the droids and voice of Chewbacca in *Star Wars*, and the voice of *E.T.*). Like the audio version of a car crash, they are simultaneously so disturbing you want to cover your ears and so intriguing you must keep listening.

Matthew, Elizabeth, Jack and Nancy go on the run, but get cornered. Pod People have quietly replaced virtually the entire population of San Francisco. There's even a helicopter being flown by some unseen Pod pilot. This is where Jack proves to be more than just a frustrated writer. He gives his wife Nancy a passionate kiss goodbye, then runs towards the foe, creating a diversion as he yells: "COME AND GET ME YOU POD BASTARDS! HEY PODS, COME AND GET ME YOU SCUM!"

Later we must suffer through watching Jack's Pod doppelganger return and try to convince his former pals to make things easy on themselves and just go to sleep. He promises that when they wake back up, things will be a lot better. Jack is accompanied by Original Gangster Pod Person Geoffrey (he was of the very first) and Pod Dr. David Kibner, who still comes off like a bit of an arrogant know-it-all (it seems at least some of the pods retain a hint of their human progenitors internal charter as well as their outward appearance). Matthew and Elizabeth beg to be let go and promise they'll never cause trouble or hurt another Pod as long as they live. But as you would expect, there's no negotiating with Pod People. This is where Kibner gives the POD MISSION STATEMENT, which includes the benevolent promise I began with: "You will be born again into an untroubled world, free from anxiety, fear, hate."

The 1956 version of the Pods were generally seen as a metaphor for the Communist threat, though the filmmakers generally denied that was what they had in mind. What's the 1978 metaphor? EST and other Seventies self-improvement movements? Reverend Sun Myung Moon and the Unification Church? Cults? Consumerism run amok? Maybe. What would the next metaphor be -- the Moral Majority of the Eighties? The PC/SJW orthodoxy of the present? With all due respect to the subtext, in this case, I find the text itself more powerful. What matters is relinquishing your individual voice. Submitting to the peer pressure of the crowd, whatever the context may be. Once you do that, you're a Pod. Or at least en route to becoming one.

Elizabeth's defiant response to Kibner's sales pitch for the Pod life is to tell Matthew she loves him. Finally, it's not unrequited anymore! Has she always loved him or was she just fond of him, then grew to love him as he rose to the dire occasion and helped her escape the Body Snatchers -- at least until now? I think she always loved him, but it took these extreme circumstances for her to put aside surface things and focus on the substance that truly matters.

Later, having escaped to the city docks, Elizabeth twists her ankle and can't walk any further. Matthew carries her until they collapse in the tall weeds. He finally tells Elizabeth that he loves her, something the audience has known for a long time, and which she may have known before the movie started. But at this point, love is not enough. Through tears of exhaustion and despair she tells Matthew she can't go on. But then something magical happens...

MUSIC.

We hear a bagpipe band droning "Amazing Grace" at maximum volume from the PA system on the deck of a big freighter docked nearby. An escape route! They can get away together on that ship! After all, it's a good bet that POD PEOPLE DON'T LISTEN TO MUSIC! And if they do, it would be Muzak, or maybe "Been To The Desert On a Horse With No Name" (no offense to the band America) -- not something as extreme and peculiar as fucking "Amazing Grace" performed by the Royal Scots Dragoon Guards! (In another odd connection to this movie, "Amazing Grace," happens to have been my father's favorite bagpipe tune, which we played at his funeral).

Matthew goes to check out the ship as the music swells with volume and emotion. It stirs the soul -- something those wretched Pod People definitely don't have. After so much edge-of-your-seat tension and back-of-your-seat terror, this scene of Matthew running alone on the dock towards the hulking freighter while the Pipes & Drums play offers an incredible relief and the promise of hope...until we see a pallet of giant Pods hoisted up to the ship's deck. The music cuts out and we hear static as some unseen Pod Person on the bridge changes the station to a monotone weather report.

A sorrowful Matthew returns to find Elizabeth asleep. He tries to wake her up but her body crumbles in his arms -- and then her stark naked Pod Person rises up from the tall weeds and beckons him to sleep. This is definitely not how he hoped it would be when he finally got to see the woman he loves with her clothes off.

And then there's the ultimate horror of an ending...

Matthew, our sole surviving human hero, walks a tree-lined path in front of San Francisco City Hall. To thirteen-year-old me, resident of the North-East, they were very strange-looking trees. So strange I wondered if they were mutant pod-trees whose trunks had been "Body Snatched." Years later, I would learn they were pollarded California sycamore trees, whose branches had been pruned, causing calluses to form over the cut-down spots. In the intervening years, I have visited them in person, and in my opinion, they remain the FREAKIEST LOOKING TREES ON EARTH. If 1978 had an Oscar for Best Location, this scene deserved it.

As Matthew keeps walking the impossible happens. Someone calls his name. He turns and sees Nancy. She too has managed to stay alive, masquerading as one of them! She approaches, unable to contain the barest hint of a smile. As she gets closer Matthew raises his arm, points a finger at her, opens his mouth wide and emits the unearthly piercing screech of a Pod Person. WHAT JUST HAPPENED? ISN'T HE THE HERO???

Nancy stands there and breaks into tears. She knows it's over, for her and anyone else left. All will be born again into an untroubled world, free from anxiety, fear, hate -- and free from the concomitant excitement, joy, love. Free from humanity. Game over, we lose.

It was a perfect ending to the story, but it was also the darkest ending I'd ever seen in my life. Even now, more than forty years later, I don't think a more absolute soul-crushing ending has ever been delivered to an audience (and the movie was still a success at the box office, costing $3.5 million and earning $24.9 million).

That Christmas Eve was the first time I saw something I recognized as the real world invaded and terrorized by something from beyond, be it supernatural or alien. This wasn't the world of *Frankenstein, Dracula,* or the *Wolfman*, with their melodrama and theatricality. This was my world, which made the story of its obliteration an order of magnitude more compelling, and terrifying. To put it in 2019 terms: my mind was blown. Looking back after four more decades of watching, writing, and making movies, I agree with those who call it the "greatest remake ever made."

I got up and walked out of the theater in absolute silence.

We all did. It had been the last show of the night on Christmas Eve, and the rest of the mall had shut down while it was playing. All the stores were locked up and the lights were dimmed. It was so empty our footsteps echoed through the cavernous space as we headed to the garage. My dad was walking in front of my brother and me, and aside from our mom, there was no one else in sight. Then without warning, dad turned around, raised his arm, pointed his finger at my brother and me, opened his mouth wide and let out a piercing unearthly screech the likes of which had never before been heard on Christmas Eve or any other night or day in the history of King's Plaza (and hopefully has not been heard since).

My brother and I screamed at the top of our lungs and ran. Then we heard our dad start laughing and realized The Body Snatchers had not come down off the screen and turned him into a Pod Person. Somehow, be it knowingly or subconsciously, this movie -- as much about the vital but fragile nature of human relationships as the threat of pods from space -- inspired him to connect with us, by terrifying us, and then making us laugh. Dad hadn't been absorbed after all. So he, our mom (who by now was also laughing), my brother and I could get in the car, drive back across the hapless borough of Brooklyn to our grimy street, and keep living in our troubled world filled with anxiety, fear and hate -- together with its concomitant chance at excitement, joy and love. Thanks to director Philip Kaufman and his talented colleagues, thirteen-year-old me had never felt happier to be alive.

HOUSEBOUND

BY
CHRISTIAN MEOLI

Movie Theater Owner/Distributor/Actor/Producer
Arena Cinelounge Hollywood, Alive, Ray Donovan
Facebook/Twitter/Instagram: @ArenaCinelounge
Instagram: @Meolila

I never experienced the paranormal until I moved to Hollywood. It's a place where spirits from yesteryear like to remain. Sometimes, if you're not careful, they'll inhabit thister-year as well. I'd heard infamous stories of certain haunted locations; the Knickerbocker Hotel, the Wax Museum, and Bela Lugosi's apartment on Harold Way.

In 2011, I began showing new movies as Arena Cinema, just off Hollywood Boulevard in the Egyptian Theatre's former 2 & 3 space, which had stopped screening films in the early '90s when The Egyptian complex was shut down by United Artists and split up (the large theater later reclaimed by The American Cinematheque). The 2 & 3 space was mainly just a small theater and off the radar until I started it up again. It had the original seats from the '70s and a deteriorated sound system. I upgraded with the budget I had, and it wasn't until I had sunk all the money I had left to show new movies that I began to realize I had a silent partner in the endeavor, who was lonely and very much watching me and wanting company.

The first encounter was inexplicable. I was rummaging the electrical room, when I heard a blast of the final eight bars from a popular Scott Joplin ragtime tune. I couldn't tell you the name of it, but I could hum it if you asked me. As I looked around the tech booth, I noticed that the sound system wasn't turned on, leaving me perplexed. The second time, I was in the theater, rushing to tighten a loose screw in one of the broken seats before letting in the audience for a show. I didn't have the right tool, so I ran upstairs to the tech booth. The tool I needed was surprisingly laying in the middle of the floor, waiting for me. I mentioned these events to the building manager, who shrugged them off. The third time, I captured the spirit in a photograph: an enormous blue orb above the stage...an orb with a face. It was then that I embraced my haunted reality and acknowledged its presence regularly and ever so slowly, respecting our co-habitancy and seeking amicable relations. It resided in the back dressing room and liked its privacy. In return, I honored its space.

The entity loved the movies, especially horror films, and as I continued to show films seven nights a week, I began to develop a stronger, stranger sixth sense of its behavior, temperaments, and likes. You could say we started to talk about films together, albeit telepathically. James Cullen Bressack's *Pernicious*, IFC's *The Human Centipede 3*, and Scott Shirmer's Found were horror films that definitely made an impact on both of us. These particular titles had hardcore horrorfiles walking out of the theater, mouths agape and stunned. It was during a late night screening of *I Spit on Your Grave III* that a guest mentioned to me they saw me watching the film in the theater with them, even though I was upstairs in the tech booth playing the film. The entity was becoming a shapeshifting doppelganger. If you don't believe me, ask the The Golden State Haunt crew about their experiences. They relayed to me during one screening that they viewed a full-bodied apparition enter the theater and watch the film with them one night. *Housebound* was the film that had the most meta-influenced impact on me. Gerald Johnstone's Kiwi horror comedy about evil spirits afoot in a family domicile brought reverberating tones to my scenario. You could say that the entity and I were CINEMABOUND. One day, I remember staring into the film's key art and, like Jack Nicholson at the end of *The Shining*, finding myself superimposed into the poster. It was one night during this engagement that I returned from Boardner's around the corner and crept back behind the screen into the entity's room and politely asked if we could sit and watch the movie together on the old couch. You could say that maybe I crossed a line, or had a little too much to drink, but at the core of the invitation was a psychological projection of my life with the entity and our relationship with watching stories. Isn't that what moviegoing is all about? When that expiration moment comes for all of us, and if by chance we get stuck here, you might think a movie theater isn't such a bad place to hang.

I get asked how do I find the movies that I run. I like to think they find me. Maybe the entity drew them my way back then. I can't tell you why Arena Cinelounge became the home for new horror movies in LA, but the entity began to communicate to me which filmmakers it liked and which it wanted to go away. Over and over again, anytime we had an a-hole filmmaker on-site, or one with an incredibly negative energy, we would have suspicious technical issues. For the sake of not getting onto someone's blacklist, we'll leave the names out of this. I have to say, the entity was intelligent, had various mood swings, and a wicked sense of humor.

In 2017 we moved into a brand new state of the art theater just five blocks away at 6464 Sunset Boulevard. Our former 'roomie' thankfully decided not to join us. It was time for me to move on and continue to expand my goals and dreams. I guess you could say I didn't want to get stuck there while I'm still breathing. The old cinema will soon be torn down for more boxy condos. Maybe the entity is still there, maybe not. Perhaps it found its way to The Egyptian Theater next door. From what I hear, they have a handful of woeful entities in residence they just can't seem to get rid of.

DAY OF THE DEAD (1985)
BY
DAVE REDA

Writer/Director
Bit Parts, Horror of Our Love, My Undeadly,
Rotting Love, Love Potion #8
Facebook: @DaveReda
Instagram/Youtube: @ElftwinFilms

It's funny, the moment someone finds out I direct horror films, they always ask, "What's your favorite horror movie?" My answer stays the same. How could I pick just one film when I love so many for so many different reasons? This is what makes the horror genre great: it doesn't have to ONLY be a horror film. Take *Shaun of the Dead*, for example (one of my favorites, by the way). It can be seen in so many different ways. It's a zombie flick, a romance picture, a buddy picture; there's action/adventure; it's scary, funny, sad, and it's all awesome! There are so many levels to it and that's just one film. With horror, you can pick and choose the experience you want to have and how much severed heart you want to put in to it. This is why even a really badly made horror film can still be a lot of fun.

Even in my films and stories, I break the traditional rules of horror because I can. In the classic Universal pictures, the monster always chased a girl or wanted a friend, but was killed for it at the end. That always bothered me as a child. So in my films, the monster gets the girl at the end. It's horribly sweet! Now how to narrow the choice down to only one film? Insanity? Haha!

I really had to think this one out and go through all the list of films that inspired my work over the years that made me the filmmaker I am today. So many greats, but for me, I kept coming back, again and again to one choice...

Day of the Dead by George Romero.

The year was 1985. A buddy and I always hit up this movie theatre that only charged two bucks to see a film on Saturday afternoons. This particular Saturday however, we saw that they were playing a horror double feature. *Demons*, directed by Lamberto Bava, playing with *Day of the Dead*, directed by George Romero. We had no idea who these guys were, as we were just two underage kids wanting to sneak into horror films for the adventure and fun of it. We bought tickets for some animated kids movie, bought our snacks, and stealthily snuck into the horror movie side of the theatre. We felt like we were defying the law and grownups to see stuff we weren't allowed to see. The truth is, it was a crappy theater. The floors were always sticky and the ushers were teenagers who didn't care what we did, ha ha!

It was exciting even before the first drop of blood. *Demons* played first and it was awesome! We screamed, we hid, we laughed, we were scared and in LOVE with Geretta Geretta! It was such a great ride and we loved every minute of it. *Demons* ended and, while the guy changed the films, a few people shuffled around. My buddy and I didn't move, though. We didn't want to get caught or miss the next bloodtastic scream. Finally, the lights dimmed and *Day of the Dead* started. We were so excited, our eyes glued to the screen to see what horribly awesome things came next! Having seen a few zombie films already, I figured it would be the same kind of thing. George Romero was telling his own story with the zombie though - the progression of the monster itself - doing the coolest thing of all. He not only humanized the monster, Bub, but even make us root for him in the end. This thought, and Bub, entranced me as I watched the film. Doctor Logan, aka Frankenstein, worked with Bub and actually got him to answer a phone call from Aunt Alecia, ha ha. Yet, in Bub's eyes, you could see the struggle, pain, and craving for life. Somehow, this monster is not a complete monster at all. A human is trapped in there somewhere. Romero expertly weaved the tale and of course, the zombies finally tore the place and everyone in it apart. In this sea of blood and gore (which for my buddy and I at the time was so disgustingly awesome), the movie's soul poured through, climaxing at the moment when Bub takes mercy on Rhodes. This guy has been a total dick to everyone, especially Bub, throughout the film. Bub not only fires a gun, he essentially euthanizes Rhodes, then epically salutes his death. Oh that salute! I was glued to my chair as Rhodes screamed, "Choke on 'em!" while being torn in two by the flesh eaters, thanks to the always amazing and awesome, Tom Savini, wizard of gore. Blood and intestines everywhere...and then Bub fires and salutes...that salute saying so much without one single word. George Romero skillfully made us love a monster who wasn't such a monster after all. The movie ended and my buddy and I scampered out of the theater to retell our adventures at school for days to come. Sherman Howard's performance as Bub always stuck with me. To this day, if you ever see me growl or do a zombie shamble, I am impersonating Sherman Howard's Bub, a deadly, shambling corpse with a soul. Thank you *Day of the Dead* and George Romero, and thank you to Bub with a zombie salute and a growl!!!

I also want to thank Christan Ackerman and everyone involved with this book. It was such an incredible honor to be asked to be part of it. I know my fellow horror peeps have grrrrreat stories to tell you! So with a bloody grin, I salute you and let you shamble on.

THE BLACK CAT (1934)
BY
WILLIAM MALLONE

Director/Producer/Writer
House on Haunted Hill (1999), *Feardotcom, Masters of Horror,
Tales From the Crypt, Freddy's Nightmares*

It's hard to imagine a more corrupt and transgressive film than Boris Karloff and Bela Lugosi's first teaming, the 1934 Universal film *The Black Cat.*

Picking a "favorite horror film" is really an impossible task, as there are so many films that I have come to cherish over the years. What *The Black Cat* has for me that other films don't is an unsettling, sensual air, and a storyline that would be difficult, if not downright impossible to get made today. When asked about it, Edgar Ulmer, who wrote and directed the film, once said, "You should never commit your fetishes to film, it's just too revealing."

I want to start by saying that this whole piece is a SPOIL-ER, so don't read it if that sort of thing bothers you. Although I honestly don't think I can give away enough to ruin your enjoyment of the proceedings, since this film is just so rich in twists and plot...but you have been warned.

The story begins with Dr. Vitus Werdegast (Lugosi) taking a train to meet up with an old "friend" (Karloff) in a small town, presumably in the Austrian countryside. During the trip, he befriends a young newlywed couple. We soon find out that Lugosi is going to confront Karloff, who is now a famous architect and has built a house on top of a mountain, which was once the scene of a terrible battle. The train ride with the couple is creepy to say the least, as Lugosi strokes the hair of the bride while the couple sleeps. Lugosi holds some terrible secret that is about to be revealed.

Heading to the local hotel in town during a storm, the bus carrying the train's passengers crashes. Only Lugosi, the young couple, and Lugosi's ox-like servant survive. Soon, they wind up at the door of architect/engineer (and did I mention SATANIST?) Hjalmar Poelzig (Karloff). Once Lugosi is alone with Karloff, he confronts him. We find out that Karloff set up Lugosi to be captured by the enemy so he would be imprisoned, and convinced his wife that Lugosi was dead so he could marry her. Lugosi, only recently released from prison, wants revenge. OKAY you may think this that is enough of a set-up for a story...but wait, there's more.

We later see Karloff in bed (yes in bed...this is pre-code) with an 18-year-old hot blonde babe. She's too young to be Lugosi's wife, and there's no sign of the wife anywhere. So what gives? We soon discover that Karloff killed Lugosi's wife years ago in a satanic ritual after she gave birth to Lugosi's daughter Karen. He then waited for her to grow up and married her. Whew!

The sexual tension in this film is palpable. The interplay between Lugosi, Karloff and the young bride and groom is harrowing. During the course of the film, we find out that Karloff is going to hold another satanic ritual where he plans to kill the groom and take the young bride for himself. Lugosi finds out about the plot and instead of doing physical battle with Karloff, challenges him to a game of chess for the bride. During the game, the young couple decides they've had enough and try to leave. When they ask if they can use the phone to get a cab, Karloff's creepy manservant states, "The phone is dead." Karloff looks at the couple with a slimy stare, then back at Lugosi to say in his most lispy and iconic performance ever "Hear that Vitus? The phone is dead...even the phone is dead."

As the ritual gets started, our young bride blurts out to Lugosi that she's met his young grown daughter Karen and that she's now Mrs. Poelzig. Lugosi goes nuts looking for her, then goes ballistic when he finds that she too is now dead at the hands of Karloff. He then discovers all of Karloff's past wives and victims are encased in plastic and hanging in the basement.

So what would you do? Well, if you're Lugosi, you hang Karloff on a torture rack and skin him ALIVE!!!! This was 1934. WOW! It just doesn't get any better than this!!!!

This film was made while studio head Carl Laemmle was on vacation. Reportedly, when he returned, he was furious, not only because Ulmer did everything he was told not to do, but because he fell in love with the script girl, who was Carl Jr.'s fiancée. Edgar Ulmer never recovered from this film or the burnt bridges he left behind. He lived out his days relegated to making B- and sometimes C-grade films. One can only wonder what would have happened had things turned out differently. This is a wonderful film with great atmosphere, and some of the best Lugosi and Karloff performances. I, for one, am very glad Edgar Ulmer decided to reveal his fetishes.

THE OMEN (1976)
BY
BEVERLY RANDOLPH

Actress/Producer/Hollywood Housewife
The Return of the Living Dead, No Solicitors,
More Brains! A Return to the Living Dead,
Caesar and Otto's Paranormal Halloween
Facebook: @Beverly.Randolph.14

Being asked, "What is your favorite horror movie?" brings terror to my soul. I sincerely hate the question because it conjures up a true discomfort for me. When asked that question, I will usually say, "Well, I hate *The Wizard of Oz*," as if that will explain my stance on watching horror. Of course it doesn't explain anything but a fear of witches and flying monkeys, but that's how frightening the darker side is for me: irrational and unexplainable. I also hate using the word "hate" but I've done it now so, moving on.

I am that one who avoids all horror movies, even if my dear friends ask me to watch the movie they have just made. I do envy the people that can watch them and enjoy their adrenaline rush (or whatever it is that keeps them coming back for more). That just isn't me.

In 1974 we went to Grauman's Chinese Theater in Hollywood and watched *Earthquake* in surround sound. This was a first with surround sound. We would often go to the drive-in and the speakers that you would put in the car always sounded terrible. So this new thing was really exciting and crazy good. Grauman's Chinese Theater is the beautiful theater that would hold all of the big Hollywood premieres in the day (and it still does). For *Earthquake*, they had fishing nets hung all around the ceiling and walls in fear that the surround sound would cause great bodily injury to the mass of patrons that flooded the theater that year. I know I kept checking the walls and ceiling the whole time. What an exhilarating experience it was to see *Earthquake* there. It was a different kind of fear, a terror of sorts, and a fright if you will, but it wasn't evil.

A few years later, in our bicentennial year of 1976, a movie titled *The Omen* was released. I was 12 years old and going to the theater was clearly, a big deal. (Yes, I've given my age away but does anyone really care anymore?) Who in their right mind takes 12-year-old little girls to see *The Omen*? In all fairness, I am sure we all begged to go and now I know who to thank for my sincere fear of horror beside my parents - the one and only Richard "Dick" Donner, director of *The Omen*.

My mother worked with Dick Donner on *Goonies* and *Tales from the Crypt*, so yes, I have met this man. I didn't realize he directed this movie until recently. How I wish I knew this way back when. I would often go visit my mother on set and would have had the opportunity to tell him what his film meant to me.

Fear is one thing, but evil is another. Something evil is going to take your soul and own it for all eternity. You can look at fear and face it, but evil and Satan, never. Watching *The Omen* gives you a dread that you are staring down Satan and rooting for good to win over evil, and you ponder which side is truly stronger. Unfortunately this time, we find that evil has hit more home runs.

The Omen starts like any horror movie does, with music and credits. When the music starts and the credits roll, you automatically start pulling your sweater up around the back of your neck and tuck your feet underneath you. The music: priests chanting in latin give a feeling they are warding off evil (or are they evil?). As the orchestra plays ominously to a heavy drum pounding with the rhythm of the chant, an out of tune church bell joins in every now and then. We can thank Jerry Goldsmith, the composer of "Ave Satani" and all the music in this film. He was thanked with an Oscar from The Academy.

The credits are a dull bone white on black and dried blood red. To the right of the credits, a shadow of a boy with his hands in his pockets casts a shadow of the cross.

Title card: Rome / June 6th - 6 AM

The movie begins with a very handsome United States Ambassador to Italy, Robert Thorn, played by Gregory Peck, being chauffeured to a hospital in Rome. He looks terribly concerned. When he arrives, he finds that his first-born child has died at birth. His beautiful wife Katherine, played by Lee Remick, doesn't know that the child has died. They've been trying for so long to have a baby. The priest that just happens to meet Ambassador Thorn in the lobby suggests that he take another child, a child whose mother died in childbirth at the very same moment his wife gave birth to their dead child. There is no family, so they would be doing a kindness and Kathrine never needs to know. A few moments later, we see Robert walk into Kathrine's hospital room carrying their new son, Damien, born June 6th at exactly 6:00 A.M. that morning.

They live their wonderful lives as Robert is given the post of Ambassador to Great Britain by his dear friend from college, the President of the United States. Everything goes swimmingly until Damien turns five.

The thing with this movie is that it doesn't throw evil in

your face. This is something that could happen to any of us. This sweet lovely couple just having a nice life. The scenes are beautiful. Their homes, Italy, Great Britain, all lovely places. Nothing tells you that evil is lurking everywhere.

Here we have the first signs of trouble at Damien's fifth birthday party. This party is the envy of all children. There is a carousel, rides, lots of friends, and food. It also has the press, business acquaintances, and of course, the photographer. A Rottweiler shows up in the bushes and stares down Damien's nanny. A few minutes later, she jumps from the roof and hangs herself, proclaiming that this is for Damien. Damien sees this along with all the guests at the party. His mother scoops him up and cradles him closely. Damien looks over to see the same Rottweiler and makes an eerie connection with it. With a cock of his curly five-year-old head, and a smile and a wave at the dog, an awakening and bond has formed. Oh my gosh, how horrific. An angelic child has clearly just switched sides.

I don't want to tell you the ending, I am terrible at spoilers. I am "The Spoiler." I like to know the outcome before it happens. I often forget and assume that everyone wants to know what happens! Sigh. I will just say that if you have seen this movie, you already know. If you haven't, you must.

The movie continues on with a new nanny magically appearing to help the family in need, the house staff leaving quickly, and THE hellhound moving in. Damien's mother proclaims that Damien isn't her child and asks Ambassador Thorn "please don't let him kill me!" A priest shows up and tries to tell Thorn what really happened the night Damien was born, and finally, the quest begins to solve the mystery to do what needs to be done. I remember that after seeing this movie we would check our heads to see if we had the sign of the devil on us.

The Omen is so flawlessly well done. It is dated, but it is good. Solid.

So now you know what my favorite horror movie is and why. Yes, it's probably the only one I've seen, but it's my favorite! If you do go see this film on my recommendation, I hope to hear from you. I love good conversation, even if it's uncomfortable.

Much love,
Beverly
Born August 10th...not even close.

"Here is wisdom. Let him that hath understanding count the number of the beast; for it is the number of a man; and his number is 666." (Book of Revelation 13:18)

THE NIGHT STALKER (1972)
BY
CYRUS VORIS
Writer/Producer
Tales From the Crypt Presents: Demon Knight, Brimstone,
Sleeper Cell, Bulletproof Monk, Kung Fu Panda

First the facts: *The Night Stalker* was a made-for-television movie that was broadcast on the ABC network on January 11, 1972. In it, a crusty, rumpled and world-weary investigative reporter, played by character actor Darren McGavin, comes to suspect that a serial killer in the Las Vegas area is in fact a real-life vampire. Apparently the movie was based on an unpublished novel by Jeff Rice titled *The Kolchak Papers*. Somehow the manuscript made its way to Dan Curtis, producer of the hugely successful daytime horror soap opera, *Dark Shadows*. Curtis hired legendary sci-fi writer Richard Matheson (a novelist, short-story writer and author of several of the best teleplays for *The Twilight Zone* and *Star Trek*) to adapt the unpublished novel. Directed by television journeyman John Llewellyn Moxey, atmospherically photographed on location in Vegas and Los Angeles by Michel Hugo with a creepy and memorably modern score by Robert Cobert, *The Night Stalker* became ABC's highest rated original TV movie, earning a massive 33.2 rating and 54 share (meaning 33.2% of all households with a TV set watched the program, while among those households watching TV at the time 54% of them watched — just by comparison the final episode of *Game Of Thrones* had a 5.8 rating!), which was unheard of for an original TV movie at the time. The film did so well it was released overseas as a theatrical feature (hence the technicality that allows me to write about it in this book) and inspired a TV movie sequel titled *The Night Strangler*, which aired in 1973, a single-season TV series of twenty episodes titled *Kolchak: The Night Stalker* which ran on ABC between 1974–75, and a short lived 2005 TV series revival, and apparently it heavily influenced Chris Carter's *X-Files*.

Based on 1972 numbers and data, about 30 million people watched that broadcast on January 11...and I was one of them.

I had just turned 9 years old in the fall of 1972 and was in the middle of 4th grade at Fairview Elementary School in Cincinnati, Ohio. My father was a social worker for the city and my mother worked part-time at the post office doing the 11pm to 3am night shift sorting mail — though she was left-handed which made it hard for her supervisors to check that she was accurately doing her job, so she was shortly fired as a "high mail- tampering risk." We had very little money and most of my TV viewing was done on a small black-and-white set. I had already become fascinated by genre material, mostly comic books and Japanese monster movies, but was now trying to stay up late on Saturday nights for local pseudo-celebrity Bob Shreve's weekly all-night horror movie marathon (Bob would routinely drink beer on air and get progressively drunker as the night wore on), lured in by old 1930s *Flash Gordon* serials, then staying awake for old Universal horror movies, *Dracula*, *Frankenstein*, *The Wolf Man*, etc. Occasionally Bob would program more recent horror titles, and I discovered the Hammer films

— garishly-colored period tales filled with busty, scantily-clad females shrieking and swooning before the likes of Christopher Lee or a young, fang-toothed Oliver Reed.

I now realize the thing almost all of these films had in common was a sense of supernatural fantasy; most of them were period thrillers taking place in old haunted houses or castles on misty hills, in British moors or small vaguely-Germanic villages, which were stalked by some nightmarish creature; with settings and moods that made them seem like gothic Fairy Tales, spooky but remote and not particularly relatable...

But what was instantly riveting about *The Night Stalker* when I sat in front of the greyish glow of our old black-and-white TV was the unmistakably contemporary opening shot of a guy in a shabby hotel room fiddling with his tape recorder and an ominous first-person voice-over talking about "cover-ups" and "political careers" (this was shortly after the *Washington Post* published the Pentagon Papers and right before Watergate broke wide, but the notion of the "powers that be" deciding what the public was allowed to know of the true events of our times was starting to percolate, even to a still-forming 9-year old mind) and finally, the chilling words spoken in that V.O. by star Darren McGavin: "Try to tell yourself, wherever you may be: it couldn't happen here."

HOLY SHIT. Here. Like in Cincinnati, Ohio?

I was instantly hooked. The movie then cuts to a hand-held, verite-style shot of an attractive blonde woman walking along the Vegas strip at night and McGavin's narration continues, as if relaying ACTUAL FACTS from a documentary or news report: "Sunday, May 16th. At approximately 2:30 AM, Cheryl Hughes was standing on the corner of Casino Center and Fremont street, waiting for her girlfriend to give her a lift home..." Then the pretty blonde walks down a dark alley as the ominous music plays, crosses from the background to the foreground of the frame, from wide- shot into close-up...

...and suddenly a hand stabs out of the darkness and grabs her by the throat!

Holy Crap.

My first "jump-scare" — and in a TV movie from 1972!

I nearly fell off my couch in fright and started watching
the TV from behind my shirt collar in rapt terror as the girl
is attacked by a shadowy man in a dark suit who seems to be
hissing. Then the story cuts to a garbage man finding her body
in a can, then to a MAIN TITLE CREDITS SEQUENCE shot
entirely from the point-of-view of the girl's dead body on an
autopsy table as surgical-masked doctors stare down at the
camera, pretending to cut her open and talk in astonishment
about how much blood she's lost, the entire TITLE SEQUENCE
played dry, with no musical score, just the stentorian voices of
the physicians and the sounds of medical equipment...

This was burned into my brain and it kept getting better
from there.

More strange murders, only explained if you (the viewer)
knew vampire lore and mythology; a body drained of blood and
found in the middle of a beach with no footprints (like someone would have to fly the body there); then a series of blood-
bank robberies from local hospitals; more murders, all featuring massive blood-loss; skeptical authorities, baffled; then an
encounter with a mysterious man-in-black, a homicidal killer
who seems to have superhuman powers, tossing cops around
like rag-dolls, even after being shot several times, point-blank.
Finally, a reluctant police department convinced by the intrepid investigative reporter-hero Carl Kolchak to issue CROSSES
and WOODEN STAKES to their officers!

The film played more like a police procedural than a horror movie, certainly not like any horror movie I had ever seen.
Dracula always had a cape and spoke with a euro accent, but
the vampire in this movie wore a simple black suit and never
spoke, just let out a nerve-rattling "HISSS"...though he did have
the Eastern European-sounding name of "Janos Skorzeny" and
according to Scotland Yard and Interpol, was born in Romania
in 1899 — leaving dumbstruck authorities wondering how a
70-year-old man could beat the crap out of several police offi-

cers and escape after being hit point-blank by several rounds of ammo.

One of the things I love about *The Night Stalker* to this day is how it references classic, old-school vampire mythology, but in a sly, subtle, updated way; the vampire being born in traditional Transylvanian territory, perhaps able to fly (by transforming into a bat?), but still vulnerable to the cross and the stake of wood through the heart. Even after Skorzeny is finally killed by Kolchak, there is an epilogue that references his body being beheaded by the Las Vegas County Coroner's Office, then cremated along with the bodies of all his victims — presumably to keep them from rising back from the dead as vampires themselves.

At the end of this 78 minutes of sheer, gleeful terror, we even have a classic 1970s downbeat ending; the truth of the "Vampire Stalking Vegas" story is covered up by the local authorities, Janos Skorzeny's criminal file has disappeared and Kolchak is fired from his newspaper job and run out of town, along with his pretty and supportive blonde girlfriend, played by Carol Lynley (who seems to be a hooker or escort, though this is never explicitly stated in the film).

Then the movie returns to McGavin in his shabby hotel room with his tape recorder and his voice-over, stating: "Try to tell yourself, in the quiet of your home, in the safety of your bed: it couldn't happen here."

I don't think I had a peaceful night's sleep for a week.

From McGavin's wise-cracking, gravelly-voiced portrayal of Carl Kolchak (laying the charming-but-constantly agitated groundwork for his soon-to-be legendary performance as the expletive-filled father in Bob Clark's now classic *A Christmas Story*) to Simon Oakland as Kolchak's initially supportive, but ultimately lily-livered editor at the newspaper, to washed-up 1950s movie star Ralph Meeker (the iconic Mike Hammer from Robert Aldrich's *Kiss Me Deadly*), to an indelibly terrifying Barry Atwater, giving a wordless performance based almost entirely on a dark, menacing screen presence, bloodshot eyes and that memorable hiss, as the vampire himself, Janos Skorzeny, looking in his black suit like the screen's most terrifying undertaker; all the acting is grounded, believable and first-rate.

I even imitated McGavin's rusty-throated performance years later while acting in a high school Shakespeare play, suddenly thrust from understudy to lead and with no idea or time to figure out what to do with the part: how about doing a crazy Darren McGavin impression in iambic pentameter? Why not? Neither my acting teacher or any of the parents in the audience ever caught on, and my performance seemed to be a big hit.

The movie features several truly terrifying sequences; a blood-bank robbery gone awry; Skorzeny effortlessly snapping the neck of a German Shepherd guard dog belonging to one of his intended victims (onscreen animal cruelty that remains shocking to this day); a showdown between the modern vampire and the modern Las Vegas police that climaxes in an underwater fight in a night-lit swimming pool; and finally a genuinely disturbing scene in which Kolchak stumbles onto a woman being held prisoner, one of the vampire's victims, left alive and tied to a bed where she is being systematically bled into an IV bag for Skorzeny to feast on, a human vending machine dispensing snacks of whole blood, no quarters required.

The next day at school, I buzzed into my 4th grade classroom and almost EVERYONE was talking about *The Night Stalker*. We were all clearly too young to have been exposed to a movie like this and of course, had it been in a movie theater, we would NEVER have been allowed to see it.

But on television it was there, free and clear of any "Parental Advisories" or "TV-MA" ratings, displayed for an unsuspecting public to view. These were the days of only three networks and maybe a PBS station and local UHF showing reruns of *Gilligan's Island* and *The Munsters* if you were lucky. Everyone watched mostly the same set of popular programs — and it seemed like EVERYONE at Fairview Elementary's 4th Grade class watched this. We all played it cool but I felt we were all thinking the same thing, Carl Kolchak's final words echoing in our nervous 9-year old heads: "It couldn't happen here..." Or could it?

This is the ultimate genius of *The Night Stalker* and why it's stuck with me for so long — it's one of the first horror movies to update the old Universal monsters, and bring them kicking and screaming into the here and now. No spooky castles or cobwebs or old dark houses; this supernatural horror stalked the back alleys and neon-soaked streets of a recognizable, contemporary American city. Polanski and Friedkin had the Devil and religious dogma to dissect, but Dan Curtis, Richard Matheson, Jeff Rice and Darren McGavin had to make due with an old-fashioned blood-sucking fiend from Romania and they faired just as well, paving the way for movies from *The Hunger* to *The Lost Boys* to *Fright Night* to *The Howling* to *American Werewolf In London* to *Buffy* to the *Twilight* series — movies that updated classic movie monster tropes to the modern day.

This movie showed me what kind of emotional roller coaster-style reactions a piece of filmed entertainment could elicit from an audience — even an audience sitting at home watching the images on an old black and white TV set with tinny, non-surround sound speakers. I have gone on to a successful career as a screenwriter, wrote a few horror screenplays myself and created a horror TV show too, all no doubt consciously or SUBconsciously influenced by the nerve-jangling, unsettling, dry news report, you-are-there style of *The Night Stalker*, its TV movie sequel and subsequent series. (To be honest though, the *Kolchak* TV show immediately threw believability out the window with its "Monster-Of-The-Week" format; just how many unearthly supernatural terrors could one intrepid reporter stumble upon, for God's sake?)

Now I am middle-aged, married, live in a big American city, have two kids who are rapidly approaching young adulthood, even a dog, and life is pretty ordinary.

But every so often, sometimes, late at night, I'll hear a strange noise (a hiss?), see a weird glint in the shadows (fangs in the moonlight?), and find myself, in the quiet of my home, in the safety of my bed, whispering: "It couldn't happen here."

T H E E N D

HELLO MARY LOU: PROM NIGHT II

BY
MICHAEL PEREZ

Director/Producer/Singer
*More Brains! A Return To The Living Dead, ROBODOC: The
Creation Of ROBOCOP, Pennywise: The Story of IT*
Instagram/Twitter: @MikeysDreamin

Flames, decay, jewels and fashion all on one VHS box cover. How could it not call out to me from across the video store?

Growing up in Kalamazoo Michigan, there wasn't a whole lot to do besides school and living 90% of my life in my imagination of achieving the American Dream...being famous.

So on the weekends I would have my mother take me to this mom-and-pop video store where you could rent three films for three days. But, of course, I had to share the choices with either my sister or friends that were staying over.

My choice was always my favorite, *Hello Mary Lou: Prom*

Night 2. Mary Lou was something I always wanted to be in life (judge me if you will) but was always too shy to be. A rebel.

Burnt alive on her prom night, she comes back years later to reclaim her crown.

Vicki, the new upcoming queen of the prom, gets possessed by Mary Lou, and suddenly everyone just starts to die in order for her to win.

Teenage pregnancy, adolescent drug use, incest, religion, locker room shenanigans, and lets not forget - a crazy, possessed rocking horse with wicked pink eyes and disgusting tongue.

This was the film I would make my friends watch over and over and I couldn't get enough. They thought I was out of my mind for loving it.

Prom Night II was so wild. The locker room death scene is just one of the awkward moments, where a possessed Vicki joins her friend in the shower. She randomly kisses her, and then chases her through the locker room, eventually crushing her with her own hiding place while humming a '50s pop tune. I mean, her friend was okay with naked pecking in the shower at first...is this something we do?! It wasn't even happening to me and I felt awkward. But whatever floats your boat.

And just when I thought this movie couldn't get any more fucked up, she flat out makes out with her father. He appears to be enjoying it and, when her mother walks in and catches them, she uses some sort or devilish telekinetic power to throw her through a door. "Like, sorry mom, I was making out with dad and you interrupted." Ha!

Someday, I want to ask the writer what inspired that scene. Seeing it with my mother made me feel all sorts of weird. It's bad enough to watch a sex scene with your parents, but to see full on tonsil hockey with the pops just causes overboard anxiety.

Movies like this were made for you to escape life and that is exactly what I did. I couldn't wait for the day I'd leave that state, so I had to bide my time with the most fucked up movie around.

What? You never wanted to set your science teacher's crotch on fire with one of the Bunsen burners in class with telekinesis? Come on!

EVIL DEAD II

BY
LEE BOXLEITNER

Writer/Director/Producer
Downstairs, Die! Sitter! Die! : Rupert, Blood Streams
Instagram: @TheLeeWithNoName
Facebook: @Lee.Boxleitner YouTube: @SonOfTron

My older brother and I are lucky enough to be able to make horror movies, and we are even luckier when we go to festivals where they're playing. In every interview we've ever done, at some point, we're always asked the same question: "What's your favorite horror movie?" Everytime, an answer flies out of my mouth without me even having to think.

Much like some of you, if not most of you, I discovered a love for horror movies at a young age. Some of my earliest memories are of hiding behind the couch as our old friend Freddy K. broke his way out of poor Jesse's chest to eviscerate his totally straight best friend, Grady. (*A Nightmare On Elm Street 2* was one of the few VHS tapes I owned at the time, but

I was three, so give me a break.)

It was on a winter's night in 1992 when I was seven that it happened. My stepmom knew that my older brother and I were forming a small obsession with all things horror and was delighted to discover that we had never seen one of her favorites. She started the Jiffy Pop and pulled out what looked like a blank VHS tape. I'll never forget that moment when she slid the tape out of its faded rainbow casing. Written on the label in thick, black Sharpie were the words, *Evil Dead II.*

From the moment it started, I was hooked. I found myself being terrified to look at the screen, but laughing hysterically moments later. I was enamoured of the practical effects by Robert Kurtzman, Greg Nicotero, and Howard Berger. My mind was blown by the wild, but masterful, camera work and direction from Sam Raimi. But most of all, I found my childhood hero: Ash Williams. I know what you're thinking, "DUH! Ash is fucking badass!" But at that time, none of my friends knew what *Evil Dead* even was. They were busy watching *Power Rangers* and *Tiny Toons* (by the way, I am in no way looking down on either of those. Trust me, I had my fair share of *Mighty Morphin* fun!), but Ash and *Evil Dead II* felt like my little secret. And I cherished that.

Needless to say, I became obsessed. My stepmom, bless (or should I say "swallow") her soul, let me keep that tape and I watched it EVERY NIGHT for months on end. I made Ash's costumes and props just to wear during my nightly viewing. I guess I was a cosplayer before I even knew what it was. I would pretend to be Ash and fight invisible Deadites in my room. Inevitably, I would wake up my mom and stepdad in the middle of the night whenever Henrietta waited for me in the fruit cellar of my nightmares. I even got my first concussion trying to flip myself over like Ash and his possessed hand!

I recently went through a great loss, so I decided it was time for some horror movie therapy. I popped in my old friend (unfortunately I don't have the VHS anymore, but DVDs are just as good!) and lost myself in the magnificence that is *Evil*

Dead II. Something hit me. While I didn't realize it as a child, *Evil Dead II* was in actuality a metaphor for life.

Let's take a look at Ash Williams. At the beginning of the film, he's pretty simple, with one goal in mind: he wants to get laid. Now, I know this sounds silly, but stay with me. Ash is a young guy just trying to have fun and live his life before the pressures of adulthood kick in. I freely admit, opening up the *Book of the Dead* and listening to the recording was a really stupid thing to do, but haven't we all made stupid decisions in life? I certainly have. How we deal with those decisions is what defines who we are.

Unfortunately, in Ash's case, his stupid decision summoned pure evil. He tries to run at first, speeding down the dirt road only to be foiled by a mangled bridge. But that's life. You can't run from it. There are "mangled bridges" everywhere! So what does Ash do? What do we do? There's really only one true option. We go back to that fucking cabin and face our lives head on. On your journey, people will come and go, just like Linda, Annie, Ed, Jake and Bobby Joe, and even though they are important to the story and can help you along the way, they can't be the ones to save you. You are the only one who's going to get you through life. (Read the Latin a little faster, Annie! Jesus!)

There will be times in our lives when things are thrown our way that we don't want to deal with, things we don't even think we have the capacity to deal with. Whether it be chopping off your own hand with a chainsaw or separating with the love of your life. (I know that sounds rather specific, but it's personal.) The point is, when life seems a little too tough - and it will - we have to be a bit more like Ash Williams: strap on that chainsaw and cut down any Deadite stopping you from living the life you want. And when that giant slimy monster head of life bursts through the front door, grabbing you with its tree hands, reminding you of all of your dead friends (mistakes and regrets), stay groovy and stab it in the fucking eye! Just don't forget your chemistry books when you get sucked back to the dark ages. You're really gonna want those...

Now I'd like to know, did you have a similar relationship with any particular film? What horror movie inspires you the most in your daily life?

P.S. REMEMBER: Deadites are not people. Please don't actually use a chainsaw to kill anyone...

KING KONG (1933)
BY
GARO SETIAN

Director/Writer/Trailer Editor
Automation
Instagram: @GaroSetian Facebook: @Garo.Setian

The original 1933 *King Kong* is not only my favorite horror film, but it happens to be my favorite film of any genre. Not only was it groundbreaking in terms of special effects and sound, but it was a perfectly structured story for a motion picture, bringing to life things that we can only see at the movies, and in the end, gets us to feel something for a fearsome creature that, for the most part, is an animated doll. It is a completely transportive cinematic experience and is the very essence of why I still obsessively watch movies and have pursued making them.

Kong wastes little time. Within the first 22 minutes we get to know all the main characters and understand what their motives are. By the 28-minute mark, we land on the mysterious Skull Island and, by the 38-minute mark, Ann Darrow is kidnapped by the island natives to be sacrificed to Kong. From there, the movie is non-stop action, spectacle, and set pieces, until the film reaches its heartbreaking conclusion. It's a hell of a ride.

King Kong has been described as an adventure and a fantasy, but it certainly qualifies as horror, especially if you look at it within the context of when it was made. It has a lot of scenes that were clearly intended to terrify audiences, with various characters being eaten alive by dinosaurs, hurled from massive heights to their deaths, and being chomped up by Kong, tossed to the ground, and then stomped on. Death is everywhere in *Kong*, and everyone goes out screaming.

Let's talk about those screams. They are some of the finest screams you will ever hear in a movie. I'm not just talking Fay Wray's heightened state of continual terror throughout the film (which is impressive), but the poor doomed crew of the *SS Venture*! In an early encounter with one of the prehistoric monsters on the island, they are eaten and tossed about by a strangely carnivorous Brontosaurus. As some of the crew escape, one guy falls behind, trying to get away by climbing a tree. That plan fails immediately as the dinosaur finds him in seconds. This whole sequence is egged on by Max Steiner's amazing score, which is equal parts horror, adventure, and sheer aggression. We watch as the helpless guy tries to wiggle away from the hungry dinosaur that almost looks amused at the man's predicament. We mercifully cut away to a wide shot when the dinosaur successfully grabs the man in his jaws. The music stops so we can hear only the man's desperate, long-winded scream. The dinosaur lowers its head to dine on the now silent man and we are treated to a loud blast of Steiner's music that suggests what we just witnessed was the most horrifying thing of all time.

Kong sends many more men screaming to their deaths shortly thereafter in the infamous "log scene," where Kong shakes the men off a log that is over a deep ravine. One after another, the men plunge to the bottom, screaming all the way down, only to be immediately cut off when they make an impact with the ground. The one guy who manages to hang on the longest is rewarded with the most violent end, as Kong just grows weary of shaking the log and tosses the whole thing down the ravine. Once again, the music stops, as we listen to the guy scream all the way down. But just before impact, he switches from his scream to an "Ooooo" sound. It's as if he managed a moment of reason beyond the terror of the fall and braced for the impact. This is immediately followed by a terrifying CRASH sound as the log smashes at the bottom of the ravine tossing his helpless little body to the ground.

As any *Kong* enthusiast knows, there was a lost "spider pit" scene where these men were then eaten alive by all sorts of horrifying creatures. Peter Jackson wittily recreated this lost scene as a special feature on the *King Kong* Blu-ray, and while more monsters are almost always better in my humble opinion, the fact that any of these guys would still be alive after that fall, even within the realm of a fantasy film like this...is highly unlikely.

After the horrors of the "log scene," *Kong* piles on one set piece after another: Kong trying to grab John as a giant lizard scales the ravine wall to eat him; the T-Rex (probably really an Allosaurus) vs. Kong fight!; the Kong vs. Tanystropheus fight; Kong versus a Pteranodon!; and, within all these sequences, one thing becomes clear to us...Kong cares for Ann Darrow. He is trying to protect her.

During the Pteranodon attack, John and Ann escape after a seriously high drop into the ocean and then a race through the jungle with Kong in hot pursuit. The set pieces keep coming when the remaining crew of the SS Venture and the natives try to keep Kong behind the large doors that have kept him out of the village for years. But Kong wants Ann back, and he pushes and pushes and breaks through the mighty doors and commences a merciless attack. Kong takes time to chew on the natives before throwing them to the ground. One poor soul not only gets chewed, but stomped face down into the mud. Others are just crushed by Kong's mighty fists. It is a non-stop parade of carnage that briefly stops when Kong succumbs to the gas bombs.

It is here that the storytelling efficiency of *Kong* really shines. Carl Denham announces his plans to take Kong back to New York in an epic show. "I can see it now, Kong the eighth wonder of the world!" CUT TO New York, and a sign announcing "KING KONG THE EIGHTH WONDER OF THE WORLD."

It isn't long before Kong breaks loose in a wonderfully stylish sequence of photographer flashbulbs making Kong think Ann is under attack. From there, Kong is loose in the city causing all sorts of damage. Through it all, there is a continuous sense of wonder to go along with the terror and thrills. We are invested in the characters (including Kong).

One particular horrifying moment that stayed with me long after first seeing the movie is when Kong reaches into a high rise and pulls out who he thinks is Ann Darrow, but it's another woman instead. Kong just drops her. We see her wiggling as she plunges what seems like many miles to her certain death. Kong eventually finds Ann, takes her to the top of the Empire State Building, and the stage is set for one more incredible set piece where biplanes try to take down Kong. And yet, it is within this action sequence that the biggest emotional crescendo of the film happens. We see Kong is doomed. As he gets shot, we experience his bafflement at being injured by bullets and his sorrow over losing Ann. You feel sorry for him. Ann has only seen him as a monster, but we in the audience have seen him as something more. And when he takes Ann into his hand one last time, while she still squirms and kicks to get away, we feel for him. He dies an Oscar caliber death, holding onto the tip of the tower till the last second, before plunging to the earth. When Carl Denham delivers the final line, "It was beauty that killed the beast." I get chills every time.

The character of Kong is a brilliant creation. A combination of various stop-motion puppets created and animated by Willis O'Brien, giant full-scale mechanical props of Kong's head, fist, and foot, and groundbreaking sound design. He is not a living being, but a construct of the filmmakers and talented craftsmen who set out to make him appear as realistic as possible. And their efforts produce something that, while onscreen, evokes fear, some laughs (Kong playing with his dead dinosaur foes is always funny), and empathy. We really feel something for this creature at the end...but he isn't real. Only through the magic of cinema are we able to experience this creature of the fantastic and feel something for him.

It was my love of dinosaurs that initially drew me to the film when it would play on television. Every Thanksgiving for many years, a triple feature of *King Kong, Son of Kong* and *Mighty Joe Young* was shown on cable. The techniques of bringing these creatures to life fascinated me. I wanted to create worlds of adventure like *Kong*, so I would research special effects in books on the making of fantasy movies, as well as magazines like *Fantastic Films*. I learned about stop motion animation and its pioneer Willis O'Brien, and later Ray Harryhausen. I wanted to be those guys!

My obsession with wanting to make movies did not go unnoticed by my family, so on my 9th birthday, my grandfather gave me an old Brownie 8mm film camera. It did not have a single frame option but I tried doing animation anyway, firing off 3 or 4 frames at a time with quick hits of the trigger. I wasn't a great model builder, but I did create my own monsters from clay and attempted animation with the camera. Those early attempts impressed my Dad enough that the following Christmas, he gave me a Super 8mm film camera with a single frame option. The animated films I proceeded to make later provoked gifts of an editing viewer and splicing tape. Soon, I was making rather elaborate homemade adventure movies with monsters and crude special effects, but with every effort, I would learn something new and the work would improve.

By the eighth grade, I became involved in public access television, learning to work cameras and, at the time, "modern" editing equipment. By my junior year of high school, I had started my own television series, *Valley of the Shadows*, a *Twilight Zone*-styled show dealing with dramatic stories of the fantastic. I would carry on this theme of fantastical stories through my film school years. At both NYU and then later USC, I made short films that would feature a little shape-shifting ball of clay with eyes I called "Blob." They were cute short movies where Blob would help out human characters with their problems. I sold one of these films to Showtime, and the others played multiple film festivals and won many awards.

Ultimately, those shorts were not going to make me much of a living, so I spent the last 20 years making a career as a movie trailer editor. Over those years, I would try repeatedly to make different features, but would often suffer the heartbreak of a lot of effort being put into projects that ultimately did not materialize. When I finally did have a solid opportunity to make my first feature, I decided to reach back to what I loved most about making movies: making the unreal real.

My film *Automation* is deeply influenced by *Kong*. It has a similar structure in terms of setting up the characters and goals and then ultimately unleashing the action. It too has a character at the center of the story that is a complete fantasy creation. Auto, (the robot in *Automation*) is a combination of a wonderful suit built by "Evil" Ted Smith and Robert Miller, a physical performance by suit actor Jeff J. Knight, a vocal performance by VO artist Jim Tasker, dialog written by myself, Rolfe Kanefsky and Matthew L. Schaffer, sound design, wonderful human performances by other actors reacting to the robot, and a haunting score by composer Joel Christian Goffin. All of these elements work toward making Auto into a fully formed character that audiences feel something for. Like Kong's doomed love for Ann Darrow, Auto's feelings for his human coworker Jenny, played by Elissa Dowling, is the heart of the movie. Early into the production, I told an interviewer, "I hope the audience finds the film funny, exciting and, if we do our jobs right, kind of moving." I humbly leave it to those who seek it out and experience it on their own to decide if we succeeded or not.

There are certain movies we watch repeatedly during our most formative years that we continuously return to throughout our lives. And even if we were to find a film equally as precious to us, we will never see that new film as many times as that one we grew up on. When you are an adult with adult responsibilities, you simply do not have time to watch movies that you used to, and when you do eventually retire, chances are you will be returning to your old favorites again. There are only so many film viewing hours in a lifetime, and when you already clocked in so many on a certain film, it is nearly impossible for a new one to catch up.

King Kong is that precious of a film to me! It started me on this filmmaking journey and has been embedded in my DNA ever since. I will always love it.

THE SLUMBER PARTY MASSACRE
BY
AMA LEA

Director/Photographer
Deathcember, ABCs of Death 2.5, Fangoria, Delirium
Instagram/Twitter: @MissAmaLea

I should start by saying that there are probably at least a dozen or so movies I could rattle off that I have a higher love for that give me the "cinema tingles," as I like to call 'em. But this particular movie has had the biggest effect on my life. I often wonder if I would have ended up where I am without this little slasher film. Would I be a feminist? Would I be a filmmaker? Would I have left my tiny hometown for Los Angeles? Would I be an artist? Probably not...and that film is *The Slumber Party Massacre.*

I grew up in Bucksport, Maine, which you've probably never heard of. It's a small town on the outskirts of Bangor, which you probably *have* heard of since you're reading a book about horror movies and, ya know, Stephen King. Maine is beautiful and spooky and, for a fourteen-year-old whose closest neighbor is at least a couple miles away, absolutely boring. Summers were spent waiting for Wednesdays. That was dollar movie night at Snowman's Market, the local grocery store, pizza place and, best of all, video store - all rolled into one. My family would give me five bucks to drop. That meant I could rent five movies if I waited until Wednesday!!!!

The horror section was vast. An entire floor-to-ceiling wall of horror VHS tapes to peruse, not to mention all of the new releases. That particular summer, I started with all of the *Nightmare on Elm Streets*, then the *Friday the 13ths*, then the *Halloween* franchise, with some really random titles in the middle like *Cemetery Man, The Nest, The Haunting,* etc. (I really chose just based off cover art if I'm being honest.) One fateful evening, I picked up *Slumber Party Massacre*. You can probably see the cover art in your head: three scantily clad girls with a dude's butt in the foreground holding a drill weapon. It looked pretty cool.

I took home my stack of movies and immediately popped them in. I remember my family was out swimming in the backyard and finding it very peculiar that I'd rather stay inside watching movies, but I'd already fallen down the horror rabbit hole and couldn't get enough. At this point, I was a rabid fan and spent most of my waking hours over the summer break digesting as much horror as I could get my hands on, or I would search the web (please keep in mind that this was the '90s, so the internet was pretty much the Wild West at this point) for horror movies I had yet to see or news about movies in production.

Anyway, back to *Slumber Party Massacre*. If you haven't seen it, I'll give you the down and dirty synopsis. The film opens with a paper boy throwing papers describing the escape of a mass murderer, Russ Thorn, who is insane and on the loose! After the opening credits roll, we settle in with Trish Devereaux-Craven (maybe an homage to Mr Craven, himself??), a high school senior, waking up, getting naked (and then dressed) and heading downstairs to see her parents off for the weekend. She decides to throw a slumber party. Their neighbor, Mr. Contant (who seriously looks the same age as the teenagers), assures her parents that he'll be around to check on the girls.

Back at the high school, Russ kills a telephone repair woman (after she's awkwardly hit on by two high school boys, Jeff and Neil) and steals her van. We cut to Trish and her friends Kim, Jackie, Diane, and several other the girls practicing basketball in the gymnasium. It's super awkward because no one is wearing a bra and I swear, the idea of playing basketball without a bra sounds like a death designed by Jigsaw. During an ultra-male-gazey locker room shower scene, we hear the girls making plans for the evening's slumber party. Trish says she plans to invite the new girl, Valerie Bates (get it, like NORMAN BATES?), but refuses after overhearing the girls gossip about her. Russ, our resident driller killer, watches the girls leave school from his awesome new van. He sees a girl going back inside the school to retrieve a book and decides it would be best to lock her inside and attack. He injures her arm, cat and mouse tropes ensue, and eventually follows a trail of blood to finish the deed.

Later that night, the party begins with the girls smoking pot and talking about boys. Meanwhile, Valerie (who conveniently lives next door) babysits her younger sister, Courtney. The lame high school dudes from earlier show up outside the slumber party and spy on the girls changing. All this happens as Russ kills Mr. Contant with his super-phallic drill. Courtney begs Valerie to go to the party, but Valerie protests. Diane makes out with John (another boy who has shown up to the party as high school boys in movies often do) in the car and gets out to ask Trish permission to go with him. When she returns, she finds him decapitated. She tries to flee, but is also murdered. Sucks to be Diane.

While the girls are on the phone with their basketball coach, the pizza guy shows up with his eyes drilled out. The coach hears the girls screaming and heads over to the house to see what's going on. The girls try calling the police, but Russ cuts the phone line before they're connected. They arm themselves with knives, while the creepy peeping tom boys try to run for help, only to be dispatched by our driller killer. Russ gains entry to the house, murders Jackie, and chases Kim and Trish upstairs. Courtney and Valerie go over to the house, but find it dark with no signs of the horror that happened. After Trish and Kim barricade themselves in a bedroom, Russ enters through a window, stabbing Kim with her own knife as Trish flees.

Courtney and Valerie find Kim dead. Russ attacks them, but Valerie escapes to the basement while Courtney hides under the couch. The basketball coach arrives and beats Russ with a fireplace poker, but he murders her. Trish stabs Russ with a butcher knife to little avail. Valerie chases Russ with a machete out the back door. She severs his drill bit and his left hand, and he falls into the swimming pool. As the girls embrace, Russ emerges from the pool and attacks them. Valerie impales him with the machete, killing him. Valerie and Trish break down into tears. Police sirens sound off in the distance.

To a fourteen year old girl (again this was the '90s so there really wasn't anywhere to read essays or hot takes or critical reviews on film without a magazine, etc.), I could tell that there was something different about this slasher compared to the others I'd been binging on all summer long, but I couldn't put my finger on what it was. I did notice right away that all of the main characters were objectified and I kept expecting them to die. But the difference was that their characters were developed. They also smoked weed, had sex, and spent a lot of time objectifying men (even looking at a stack of *Playgirls* at one point.) Now this was shortly before *Scream* came on the scene, but by this point, I was already versed in the slasher rules: If you drink, fuck or do drugs, you're gonna die. But AGAIN, this wasn't the case for *Slumber Party Massacre*. Even though I couldn't process what all this exactly meant at the time, you better believe that fourteen-year-old Ama TOTALLY got it when Valerie machetes the killer's big long drill in the final battle. I cheered out loud to myself at the emasculation of our killer. What an ending!

After the final shot with the girls in shock and crying and sirens wailing in the distance, let me tell you what this essay is really all about: seeing those end credits for the first time. Directed by Amy Jones. Directed. By. Amy. Jones. A woman. This was the first time I'd ever seen a woman's name as the director of not just a horror movie, but of ANY movie. I don't think there was ever a thought in my head that only men could make movies, but moreso, I had never really thought about it as something women did...that it was something I could do. I knew I loved horror movies. Did I want to pick up a camera and make my own? Wow...yeah. I think I could really like that.

So I watched it again, this time with a critical eye. I looked for the differences of what a slasher film looked like in the hands of a woman versus in the hands of a man. There were women in jobs usually held by men - a phone repair woman, a female basketball coach, etc. Our killer, Russ Thorn, doesn't wear a mask. He doesn't have supernatural abilities. He's actually pretty "normal", not even having an overly large physique. Could this decision be because men generally have the ability to commit acts so heinous that they don't need all the bells and whistles to be terrifying to women? As an adult woman, I can tell you the answer is: absolutely. Were the women naked, having sex, doing drugs, and then not killed because the director was trying to say that women are living breathing sexual beings just like men? Well maybe, but probably more likely producer Roger Corman required there to be some sort of nudity and Jones did the best she could with the parameters she'd been given. Instead of one "final girl," we had three. Could that mean, if women work together, they can persevere? Back to the giant drill that obviously symbolizes the killer's dick. There is an absurdly creepy line right before the end where he tells Trish, "you know you want it, you'll love it" as he inches the murder weapon toward her. Upon this second viewing, I distinctly remember the feeling I got when I heard this. If the drill really is a metaphor for his dick, then when he says this he's really saying "I'm going to rape you." It was the feeling you get riding an elevator that descends too fast and your guts feel like they are in your throat. A brief "oh" was all I could exclaim.

I didn't return this movie with the rest of my stack that week. I told the kid behind the register that regrettably, I lost it. I began watching it after every slasher movie I saw, looking for differences, trying to understand why I only had one movie out of hundreds that was made by a woman. Like there must be some secret to this. I didn't understand it or exactly what I was looking for, but I knew I wanted to see MORE movies made by women.

It's also worth mentioning that this movie was written by Rita Mae Brown. Upon researching her, a whole can of illuminating worms opened. Maine was a very sheltered place to grow up. In general, it's a pretty liberal state, but it's also super, super full of white people. I had never thought about discrimination in any sense of the word. Nor had I thought about power dynamics or entitlement or politics between the genders. I didn't even know what a feminist was or even why the movement was needed until this. I began reading her books and essays and in doing so, found so many core beliefs that I hold to this day.

That summer, I borrowed my grandfather's giant VHS camcorder - you know, the kind that sat on your shoulder and held an actual full-sized VHS tape. I began to write and make movies with my cousin and the neighborhood kids that were mostly set in my backyard. I made my movies in sequential order, rewinding and deleting scenes to edit in camera. Then, eventually, I got the idea to edit between two VCRs. We had two because my dad was like the original movie pirate, renting films and then taping them with his second VCR so he could add them to his movie collection. I got better and better at this. Not just over that summer, but many to come. I went from being an "indoor kid" to being a slightly more social "sorta outdoor kid" (well, as long as I could film something). I saw *Slumber Party Massacre* almost exactly twenty years ago and because of that movie, I picked up a camera. In the twenty years since, I haven't put it down. I am a director and a feminist because of this super tiny, low-budget slasher film. I am a stronger woman because of Amy Holden Jones and Rita Mae Brown. I owe so much of who I am as a person to this satirical slasher film and that's why *The Slumber Party Massacre* is my favorite horror movie.

FRIGHT NIGHT (1985)
BY
JACK ULRICH

Managing Editor/Screenwriter/Journalist
Tom Holland's Terror Time
Facebook: @Jack.Ulrich.549
THTerrorTime.com Facebook: @THTerrorTime

"We'll drift through it all, it's the modern age"
"These Days" by Joy Division

I am way behind in turning in this essay. It's high school all over again. Everyone around me is passing up their semester projects, while I sit in my desk trying to look engaged in the whole process when I know damn well, all I have is a handful of fucking index cards and a vague idea. But now, as then, I'll just keep slogging forward, hoping the end result is enough to generate a reprieve from ramifications.

The task was to select a horror film that had most influenced my life or had the biggest impact on how I viewed horror or just blew up my skirt in some hitherto unknown way. Easy, but not easy. Our memories of an event are recontextualized with the clutter of who we are today that we drag back into our own past.

Before I even began writing this article I told the editors that I'd cover 1985's *Fright Night*, a film written and directed by my friend Tom Holland, starring Chris Sarandon, Roddy McDowell, William Ragsdale, Amanda Bearse, Stephen Geoffreys, and Jonathan Stark. A wonderful film about a horror fan named Charlie Brewster (Ragsdale), who believes his new next-door neighbor, Jerry Dandrige (Sarandon) is a vampire. My plan was to spin a tale about the first time I saw it in the theatre and the ever-lasting impression it made on my young mind. But try as I might, I could not clearly remember the experience of seeing it for the first time. I know I liked the film; I must have, I bought it on VHS when it came out, and I rarely bought movies. Outside of creating an outright fiction, I had nothing.

So here I am again, clutching index cards…

About ten years ago I met Tom Holland and we've become friends over the years. We've travelled together to conventions, screenings, and other personal appearances. I have also worked on his social media and web presence to bring him into the 21st century. Through all of this, I have had a chance to meet not only the remaining cast of *Fright Night*, but also the die-hard fans of the film. I've been privy to some great behind-the-scenes stories and the adoration the fans of this film still heap on it all these years later. It's through these experiences that a true, honest opinion of *Fright Night* began to take form and evolve into something worth writing about.

It's an opinion that doesn't come from some wide-eyed version of myself sitting in a dark theater experiencing something magical for the first time. Rather, it comes from an exposure to not just the film, but the stories behind the making of it, as well as the impact it has had on innumerable people's lives.

At its core, *Fright Night* is a slightly bent version of Aesop's fable "The Boy Who Cried Wolf". The story of an inveterate liar who, following a series of false cries for help, is left to face a real threat when those around him grow weary of his constant deceptions. In the case of *Fright Night*, you have young Charlie Brewster, an avid horror fan, whose belief that a vampire is living next door to him and killing young girls, is chalked up to his love of horror movies and an overactive imagination. This particular thematic element is a particular favorite of Tom's, appearing in both *Cloak & Dagger* (1984) and *Child's Play* (1985).

As an adult, I noticed something I most certainly wouldn't have gleaned the first time I saw this film. Charlie Brewster is not the hero of this film, any more than John Wayne's Sheriff John Chance is the hero in the Howard Hawks film *Rio Bravo* (1959). In *Rio Bravo*, it is the character of "Dude", a former lawman turned town drunk, played by Dean Martin, that is the actual hero. Dude must overcome his crippling alcoholism and recover his dignity in order to confront a group of outlaws who are attempting to break one of their number out of the local jail.

In similar fashion, it is the character of Peter Vincent in *Fright Night* that experiences the true hero's journey. From the outset, Charlie is fully prepared to confront the evil living next door, by telling his friends, going to the cops to report the murders, and even enlisting the aid of local television horror host, Peter Vincent, to aid him in his fight. Charlie's path is clear. On the other hand, Peter Vincent is a fraud - a washed-up ham actor who only played a fearless vampire slayer in "B" grade horror films. It is Vincent who must put aside his fear and doubt to embody a role for which he is woefully miscast. It is this familiar, heroic transformation that endears Peter Vincent to millions of fans of the film, making him one of its most beloved characters. And consequently, why the 2011 remake failed so miserably: David Tenant playing Chris Angel while trying to shake off the mannerisms of the 10th *Doctor Who* just doesn't stack up to a Peter Vincent with real human flaws and the strength to overcome them.

Fright Night is just a well-crafted story with likable, identifiable characters who could easily exist in the world outside the theater. It was written long before the current trend of lazy storytelling where cliché cardboard standees take the place of characters who are then dropped in harrowing situations and creatively eliminated to sate our collective bloodlust. The characters in *Fright Night* aren't random victims forced into survival scenarios by the filmmaker. Instead, when they are confronted with the existence of evil, they pursue it to their own potential detriment. It's a horror movie about the struggle to defeat evil and heroism; concepts sadly out of fashion in these days of cynical gray morality.

DAWN OF THE DEAD (1978)
BY
STEPHEN IMHOFF

Special Make-Up Effects Artist
Excision/All That We Destroy
Instagram: @StephenImhoffMUFX
Twitter: @SomewhatFragile

Any horror fan—or movie buff in general—always has a "Top 10 List." But now, with new films coming out every week and new talent being discovered just as frequently, that "Top 10" is always in flux. When asked about my favorite film, I always tend to go to the "Desert Island" question: if I was stranded on a desert island and I could only bring one book, one album and one movie, what would they be?

The Book: *Catching the Big Fish* by David Lynch.
The Album: *The Fragile* by Nine Inch Nails.
The Movie: George A. Romero's *Dawn of the Dead.*

I discovered George A. Romero's *Dawn of the Dead* on VHS when Anchor Bay re-released it in 1996. After that first viewing, it quickly became a favorite. Then, as time (and age) went on, it became *the* favorite. It doesn't try to give you a fly-on-the-wall perspective of the chaos like so many other films. From the first frame, you're dropped into the middle of a panicked newsroom covering the epidemic taking over the world; you're thrown in with a SWAT team dealing with the problem in an apartment building; then in a helicopter escaping the chaos. And finally, you're with the main characters, as they attempt to create their own modest civilization in the famous Monroeville Mall. The jolt of energy the film gives you as it unfolds tells you, "Forget what you think the rules of a normal horror film are, because none of that is going to apply here."

Even when the film decides to take moments of relaxation, you can't help but feel what the main characters are feeling, and find yourself thinking the same thoughts as they are: How long is it going to take before the undead find their way into the mall? How are they going to survive all of this? And, when you find out that Gaylen Ross's Fran is pregnant, you find yourself sharing her unspoken anxiety. What's going to happen when Fran finally has the baby? Very few films have ever gotten me to think that way, especially after watching it multiple times.

The makeup and effects by Tom Savini left a life-long impression on me. So much so, that I ended up going to his makeup school in Monessen, PA; right outside of Pittsburgh. It was just a short distance to the Monroeville Mall, which I of course visited frequently. How could I not? The place was my church. Savini created so many iconic gore gags and zombie designs, all of which are still being referenced to this day. There's the helicopter zombie who, upon first watching the scene, immediately makes you think, "He's going to get shot dead by Ken Foree," but instead, we're treated to a legendary gore gag, as the zombie is scalped by the helicopter rotor. I never saw that coming (neither did the zombie for that matter). The Hatchet Zombie, played by Leonard Lies, was a fantastic education in how effects, editing and great acting can all work together. When Scott Reiniger's Roger succumbs to undeath, it's heartbreaking and chilling at the same time. Witnessing our dear Roger go from a tough soldier to a confused, dying man, only to then wake up as an emotionless zombie, rips me apart every time I see it. And how can you just not be astounded by the collaboration between artist and actor when David Emge's Flyboy turns into a zombie? The makeup, along with his one-of-a-kind walk (does he even notice, as a zombie, that he is still holding a gun?), set the bar for actors playing the undead to a new level.

The soundtrack Goblin composed for the film is a prime example of the power music can give to an already stand-out piece of cinema. It's as multilayered as the film itself. You experience the epic scope of the narrative when listening to the track "L'alba Dei Morti Viventi," and feel a sense of urgency when the track "Zombi" starts. But, when the library track "The Gonk" cues up, the tone of the film completely shifts to lighthearted (a music cue that was also used in Edgar Wright's *Shaun of the Dead*, which is another personal favorite of mine).

Now, let's talk about the fact that Romero (who began the "of the Dead" saga with the black-and-white documentary styled *Night of the Living Dead*) decided to not only go with color for *Dawn*, but he used a very rich color palette. From the first frames as Fran wakes up against the red carpeted wall, we are overwhelmed with color. I've always not only taken that as a sign that we're getting a completely different looking movie than *Night*, but also a far more graphic and gory film. I feel that Director of Photography Michael Gornick is never given enough credit for his use of lighting. Sometimes, the zombies are gray and sometimes they're blue. As a viewer, this tells me (without literally telling me) that all of these zombies are not from the same place. Some might be from miles and miles away, while others might have been natives of Pittsburgh and just led the "out-of-towners" to the mall because, as Ken Foree says: "They're after the place. They don't know why, they just remember...remember they want to be in here". Gornick's cinematography during the motorcycle gang's invasion of the mall should be shown to anyone who decides to pick up a camera for a career. During all the chaos, the camerawork keeps you focused exclusively on what's important, and you never get confused or distracted by anything. Romero & Gornick were in sync while shooting every frame of the movie and it shows.

There are very few films that make me want to analyze, learn, study and collect like *Dawn of the Dead*. As a collector of memorabilia from the film, I own multiple versions of it on DVD, VHS and even laserdisc, I have a signed poster by Romero, Savini, and the main cast. I own the soundtrack and library music on vinyl and, of course, multiple types of apparel (they make *Dawn* socks now). But my prized piece would have to be a tattoo of the famous face logo from the poster with Romero's signature and his "Stay Scared" quote above it. I remember when I asked him to sign a blank card so I could get it inked on me. He looked at both sides of it and asked "Why?" When I pulled up my sleeve to show him the logo, he smiled, threw his hands up in the air and just laughed. You could just tell from that moment that he really loved his fans and their devotion to his work. I don't have any other signatures inked on me and I'm not sure if I ever will. It's one of those things to remind me of how much Romero, the film, and the horror community mean to me. Because of that film, I wanted to create things; gory and beautiful things. Because of that film, I wanted to have a career in the arts/entertainment industry. Because of that film, I moved out to California, which led me to meet a group of friends that are my family, and led to me getting married. Every time I wake up in the morning, I walk into my living room and see the poster framed hanging on the wall and I can't help but think, "Where would I be if that movie didn't have such an impact on me that grew over the years and was the springboard for who I am today?"

In closing, I just want to say to Mr. Romero, thank you to the cast and crew, and to everyone else involved in getting this masterpiece made. This film is important, not only to me, but to so many others as well.

Oh, and did I mention that my wife's name is Dawn?

MISERY
BY
CHARLES CHUDABALA

Actor/Host/Producer
Ugly Sweater Party, Fameless, 2 Jennifer
Instagram: @CharlieChudah
Twitter: @CChudabala

My favorite horror movie of all time is Stephen King's *Misery*. As crazy as it might sound, *Misery* defined a giant chunk of my childhood. I was 8 years old when it was released and I remember watching it for the first time with my family after returning from a routine trip to Blockbuster Video. I was instantly glued to Kathy Bates' performance as Annie Wilkes, watching with a combination of fear and awe, shocked at what I had just seen. It was normal for me to have nightmares after watching any horror movie, but this night, my nightmares were replaced with obsession. I was obsessed. I woke up, rewound the VHS tape, and watched it again. I watched it over and over and over. *Misery* was my plaything, my toy, and my pretend game.

I studied the film, played the film, and paused the film. I wrote down all the dialogue from my favorite scenes, rehearsed them and performed them for...myself. There is a scene where Annie abandons the wounded author, Paul Sheldon, sitting helpless in his wheelchair. Her mood ranges from sarcastic storytelling to hysterical frustration. As a curious child with lots of energy, playing out these scenes proved cathartic and possibly stabilizing. I'm pretty sure I went undiagnosed for ADHD. My cure was *Misery*.

At school, while all my peers would obsess over Gushers fruit snacks, all I talked about was *Misery*. I would ask my friends, "Have you seen *Misery*?" They always replied "What's that?" I was alone in my newfound interest, but not when I was around my aunts and uncles. They loved to watch me perform magic shows, so it was a surprise to them when our regularly scheduled magic show was cancelled and replaced with monologues from *Misery* performed by an 8-year-old Charles Chudabala. They laughed, they clapped, and asked me to do it over again. I was such a ham, you could honey roast me. I happily obliged to an encore performance.

Today, I am an actor who plunged into his passion: Horror. While writing this essay about my favorite horror movie, I'm having an epiphany for the very first time. I suddenly understand why so many of my life choices have been potentially linked to this childhood favorite of mine. After my first semester in college, I abandoned my love for acting to pursue a career. Per my family's strong encouragement, I changed my major to psychology. I always thought I chose this major because it just happened to be the next class I took after my parents gave me the talk. I remained on this path with a 10+ year career as a therapist, life coach, and family consultant. I guess you could say that I developed a new passion for something I was good at, or you could you say that maybe, deep down inside of me, I wanted to understand what made Annie Wilkes tick. Why did she have such extreme mood swings? Why was she suddenly so violent one minute and then so compassionate the next?

How could these two main characters rely 100% on each other for survival and companionship, but then become the threat of each other's demise? I was a very curious child. It turns out, I was an even more curious adult.

In 2015, I made the decision to jump full force into acting again. I left my career behind in pursuit of playing characters in horror films who struggle between a fight for survival against direct threats and sometimes, supernatural forces. Ironically, the very first feature film I was cast in was called *Survive*. I have played many different characters throughout the years. Each with a unique internal battle, a different worldview, a different "tick". I'm enjoying the ride in my horror career and I'm convinced that there are no coincidences. I'm doing what I love in this genre for a reason. I have always said that horror was my safe place. The horror genre allowed many types of stories to be told from people in all walks of life. I found my community of acceptance. Annie Wilkes was not inherently bad. Sure, she had some darkness, but she was also genuinely excited to have someone to connect with, especially when that someone was her favorite author. Maybe she was just misunderstood. Aren't we all just seeking to be understood? To be "gotten?" I feel way more aligned with my true self and more connected with others with each piece of art I produce. Could it be possible that I'm playing a small part in *Misery*'s return? All I know, right now, is that *Misery* impacted my life and might be the reason I'm here today, writing this.

INVITATION ONLY
BY
JP OUELLETTE

Filmmaker/Board Game Designer
All The Creatures Were Stirring, Captured, The Dust Storm
Twitter/Facebook/Instagram: @GenreGameLabs

Discovery is my favorite part about being a genre fan. The ultimate thrill is finding a new movie (or even a classic that is just new to you) and that movie becoming an instant favorite.

This film found me later in life (as it will you), but its timing was perfect, as the recommendation to watch it came while doing extensive research for an Asian horror project. I am now pleased to be the one putting it on your radar. Ever since humanity has crossed the saturation point of visual content, I often don't spend my time watching a film unless it has been personally recommended.

The need for vetted reviewers, podcasters, and fellow fans (creating online lists, and poignant essays like the ones in this book) is more important than ever to help separate the great from the good, and especially the good from the bad. Our beloved genre has been watered down more than our opinion of it. We have been slipping.

The love/hate, thumbs up/thumbs down, "quick soundbite reviews" leave us drowning in hum, often leaving the LOUDEST person with the correct opinion unfortunately...with just one post, a film can be boiled down to being insignificant, or even worse, lumped into the "everything is everything" category, invalidating the person recommending the film because every film they post about is the best, or "everything." But how can that be??? It can't. A gem like *Invitation Only*, a heavily thematic, yet vicious, international slasher, couldn't ever fight its way through that type of noise.

We have even created a culture where constructive criticism is dead. One reviewer that I love now only does critiques of new films that they've enjoyed, skipping the disliked ones in order to avoid backlash or threats. Those same BOISTEROUS voices want to keep political commentary and thematic elements out of the genre. Which films are they watching?! Exercising your personal demons and fears into art is the genesis of the horror genre.

It has just been of late where the masses have caught up to us addicts (ironically because of the evil world that has formed and because people have been missing the point), but that doesn't stop them from being "right" as they yell into the echo chamber that is the internet.

There is a virus eating its way through the horror community in the way of popularity and adoration.

The hierarchy has been set and classism reigns.

The characters of *Invitation Only* go through that same struggle. Thematically, our hero is so obsessed with greed that he is blinded by the game set up by the elite members of society, who love toying with the poor. I love any plots driven by games, hence my social media handles.

Saw, *The Purge*, and *The Collector* franchises all have fun and games elements, and they are packed with theme, as with this film. Seek out *Invitation Only* if you're a fan of the afore-mentioned titles, it's a great companion piece.

The impact that this story had on me (and my career) was that it contained an actual message within the genre to spread that word. The homogeneous countries in Asia have extreme classism issues and caste systems that the western world needs to be aware of, and there isn't a more creative way to hide that moral than in a gore fest!

This film inspired me to focus on making horror films that have a deeper meaning. When writing or producing a new project, the first thing I ask myself is, "Will this make a difference?" Will this make the genre better? Will the audience discover and share this story? The cream rises to the top.

America has a racism issue. It has many, many, many, issues. But the outside world wants to know why we hate and how that hate affects our citizens. Artists like Jordan Peele and Ernest Dickerson are telling our unique stories and themes that are traveling around the world, in the same way this film traveled here.

Invitation Only could easily be adapted in the U.S. to reflect the topic of racism head-on in the same way the original took on classism in Taiwan; and THEME TRANSLATES. It was the country's first ever slasher/torture game flick and it was a box office hit!

Great films fight their way through to being seen. The more woven the allegory, the more deeply the film will resonate with a potential audience and open itself up to be discovered, even if it takes over a decade.

That should be our common goal while progressing the genre.

EVENT HORIZON
BY
ERLINGUR THORODDSEN

Director/Writer
Child Eater, Rift, Into the Dark: Midnight Kiss
ErlingurThoroddsen.com
Instagram/Twitter: @Lingur

Sometimes, when it comes to events that make an indelible impression on your life, context is everything. I was thirteen years old when my uncle snuck me into a late night screening of *Event Horizon*. This particular movie had a very strict "no one under the age of 16 will be allowed inside" policy, which, of course, guaranteed that I became aware of its existence and was hellbent on seeing it. I didn't know the plot and hadn't seen a trailer, but the promise of infinite space and infinite terror was enough to get me excited to see it. My parents wouldn't take me and I was too scared to go alone, so I figured I'd just have to wait for the VHS. Then, one dark and stormy night, I received a phone call from my uncle. "I'm taking you to see *Event Horizon*," he said. "Don't tell your mom."

Even with the highly publicized age restriction, my uncle (who was in his mid-twenties at the time, and largely responsible for any horror and sci fi films I'd seen so far) thought we could pull it off. Being a pessimist at heart, I wasn't so sure. We would be stopped by the ticket collector who would unceremoniously throw us out. I was not a mature-looking thirteen year old. No way in hell could I pass through without being noticed. Even as we headed to the theater, I didn't really think I'd be able to see this film I was absolutely not allowed to watch tonight...precisely because it was so forbidden, however, I knew we had to try.

There were a lot of people at the theater that night. Although *Event Horizon* would ultimately be considered a flop at the time of its release, it had a very strong opening weekend in Reykjavik, Iceland, for whatever it's worth. I assume the promise of hardcore horror (not for the faint of heart) was enough to entice the young people in typically uneventful Reykjavik to go out on a cold fall night.

So, we arrive and my uncle buys us the tickets while I hide away in a corner somewhere. His friend was with us, and the way I remember it, the friend was the one most obviously paranoid about me not getting in. He didn't want to waste his hard-earned money on a ticket only to be thrown out…

We got in line. Up ahead, I saw the ticket collector. It seemed like the line was endless. It moved ultra slowly. I barely said a word. I was too excited and nervous to speak, and I also didn't want to give myself away. I felt that everyone around us was looking at me and had clocked that I was not supposed to be there. What if someone would inform the ticket collector that a child was in line to see this evil, forbidden movie? What if there was a snitch in our midst?

We edged along slowly until, finally, it was our turn to show our tickets. I remember looking down at the floor the entire time. There was a long pause. I could feel the ticket collector looking at me. I could feel him knowing I wasn't supposed to be there. I like to imagine that some sort of telekinetic communication passed between my uncle and the ticket collector. "Please, let us through," my uncle perhaps pleaded without saying a word. "This kid loves horror. *Aliens* is his favorite movie of all time, and I showed him that on VHS. This is my chance to show him a space sci-fi horror film in an actual theater. You must let us through..." (Incidentally, not too long after this, my uncle took me to see *Alien Resurrection* in this very same theater...but that film had no strict age-policy and was memorable only in terms of disappointment.)

Nothing was happening. Why weren't we moving? This was going to fail, I could feel it. And then...my uncle's hand was on my back, pushing me forward. Somehow, it worked! We were stepping into the theater proper. I was about to watch *Event Horizon*. "You want some popcorn?" my uncle asked me, and I nodded yes. Even before the film started, I was hopped up on adrenaline. I was so jazzed. I'm sure no matter how the film would have turned out, I probably would have loved it ...

But I'm not sure a lesser film would have stayed with me for two decades the way *Event Horizon* has.

The truth is, I was in no way prepared for what I was about to see. I don't think anyone in that packed theater was, either. Certainly not my uncle, and most certainly not his friend, who was visibly shaken by the time the film ended. I don't recall there being a lot of noise during the screening. I don't remember any screams, although there may have been some. I do remember the audible gasps and muttering of horror and disgust after the crew of the Lewis and Clark finally managed to watch the last video recording made by the crew of the *Event Horizon*: an orgy straight from hell.

Laurence Fishburne's (amazing) line directly following that moment — "We're leaving" — now plays as comic. Intentionally comic, I believe — I think Paul W.S. Anderson was very aware of the fact that when playing with extreme horror the way he was, you need moments of levity to even things out. But no one laughed at my screening. People were too shocked. I had never seen anything like that before. The closest thing to this sort of dirty, dangerous horror that I had seen was Wes Craven's original *A Nightmare on Elm Street*. That had left a mark on me, but this felt even more extreme. Being in a theater no doubt added to the experience. Even though I had become a bona-fide horror devotee by this time (seeing Craven's *Scream* the previous year was a major turning point), I think the dark nihilism of *Event Horizon* steered my love for the genre in a certain direction.

Is *Event Horizon* my ultimate favorite horror film of all time? Perhaps not. There are so many films I could mention (I already managed to sneak a couple of them into this short essay), but so much has been said about those films over the years, what could I possibly add? In thinking of what film I should pick, I thought of the films I return to the most. *Event Horizon* is a movie I put on regularly, probably in an attempt to feel just a touch of that initial thrill I felt back in 1997. It is a film that was not particularly well received upon its release, but has slowly and steadily garnered a cult following and renewed appreciation. It is by no means perfect, but in terms of its concept, brilliant production design, the execution of its key set pieces, and the performances of its cast...it is kind of a perfect storm of sci-fi horror. A perfect raging Neptune storm, if you will.

Today, most of the discussion on *Event Horizon* revolves around the lost treasure trove of deleted scenes, or sharing memes of crispy Sam Neill spouting immortal lines of dialogue ("Where we're going, we won't need eyes to see."), but for me, every time I think of it, I am transported back to being a thirteen-year-old kid in a dark, packed theater, watching something I was not really supposed to be seeing, and feeling a sense of collective dread that I had never felt before in my life...and don't really think I have felt ever since.

After the film ended, my uncle looked shell-shocked. His friend was freaked out. He thought he had shown me something that would damage me for good. (He may have been right about that, I guess). That night, I couldn't sleep. It wasn't just because the film scared me so bad (which it most certainly did) - it was also because I kept replaying scenes in my head. I wanted to know more. What was the unknowable dimension the ship had been in for the past seven years? What did I actually see in those glimpses of hell that burned into my retinas in high-intensity quick cuts? When would I be able to see this film again?

Yes, the context of when and how I saw *Event Horizon* is key to how I feel about it today. But regardless of whatever flaws it may have, a film that is so viscerally thrilling and so intriguing in its mysteries of the unknown is kind of a miracle, isn't it?

I think so. A little nightmarish miracle that I know I'll keep returning to for years to come. To paraphrase Sam Neill's Dr. Weir, I can't leave. She won't let me. Just like *Event Horizon* won't let the rescue crew escape, it also has a hellish grip on me.

A NIGHTMARE ON ELM STREET
(1984)
BY
MICHAEL COULOMBE
Writer/Director/Podcaster
Soundbite, Stalk, Love Me Not, Axe, Ad Out,
Mimosas with Michael Podcast
Instagram: @MCoulombe Twitter: @MichaelCoulombe
MichaelCoulome.com

When people ask me what my favorite horror film is, I always answer quickly with *A Nightmare on Elm Street*, because - well, that is the truth, it IS my favorite horror movie. While we were growing up, my cousin Daryl always made me watch the *Friday the 13th* series. So, I do love this series, but as a kid it always terrified me...and I remember lying in my bed at night completely petrified, unable to move, praying that the sun would come up soon so I could get up and run to the bathroom. (Looking back on, it is no wonder I pee so much now!)

Now, even though these films haunted me I always loved

watching them – just don't tell my cousin Daryl. I remember
having a slumber party with all my friends when I was younger
and asking my mother to rent us *Friday the 13th Part 5*. That
was one of my favorites in the series. I do find it interesting
though that in this point of my life, Victor Miller, who wrote
the original *Friday the 13th* would not only become my friend
and mentor, but that we would also write a film together (*Eden
Falls*).

I grew up in Orange County, CA and that my childhood
house was haunted. I truly, truly believe that because Daryl,
my twin sister Michele and I heard a voice one time. We were
playing in one of the rooms and we heard a dark sinister disembodied voice tell us to 'Get Out!' We ran so fast into the living
room where my parents and Aunt and Uncle were sitting. For
the record: to this day I am terribly afraid of the dark. I do feel
that this accounts for the reason I am obsessed with haunted
houses and the supernatural!

Somehow, the fear I had for watching horror films changed
when I first saw Freddy Krueger in *A Nightmare on Elm Street*.
His face was burned and the movie was scary as shit, but I
loved the film. I loved his humor. I was an instant fan. I even
had a huge *Nightmare on Elm Street* poster hanging on my closet door. I was nine years old – I probably shouldn't have been
such a big fan at that age!

Perhaps living with a ghost made me curious. Either way, I
was drawn to the types of films that dealt with things that were
unseen to the human eye, but with *A Nightmare on Elm Street*,
I don't know, you had this bad guy who didn't just attack you in
your house - he attacked you in your dreams, the one place you
felt safe, vulnerable. I mean, how fucked up is that?!

Also, let's be honest, Johnny Depp was hot in the movie.
Who didn't love the crop top jersey he wore before his death
scene? (What a death scene, am I right?) And as a young gay
kid growing up, how can I not talk about how pivotal the sequel with Mark Patton was, with its homoerotic moments. I
mean, hello? Little did I know how that film would give me the

strength to finally come out!

The best thing about *A Nightmare on Elm Street* is that the film still scares me to this day. I think that is a testament to true storytelling. At Texas Frightmare in 2019, I was sitting at the bar at the Hyatt DFW and saw Robert Englund having a drink. There were other fans around him, so my friends and I joined him, drinking wine, and just talking. He was so animated, instantly captivating me with his stories. Eventually, my friends trailed off to check into the convention, so Robert and I sat there by ourselves for 20 uninterrupted minutes, talking about film, life, and our careers. It was a very humbling experience for me as an *Elm Street* fan, and as a horror director and writer.

The truth is, *A Nightmare on Elm Street* was one of the biggest reasons I wanted to be a storyteller. I wanted to write stories - and eventually movies - that made me feel like I felt when I watched that film; to be truly terrified. I mean, isn't that the reason we watch horror films?!

I am glad that I get to make horror movies now and find new ways to terrify audiences! In the case of *Horror House*, this was a great opportunity to create a channel dedicated specifically to horror, where I could direct films that I knew an audience would enjoy! Plus, we could focus on diversity - both in front of and behind - the camera. Teaming up with producer Ray McCann and my writing partner Brantley J Brown (who writes kickass scripts) I was confident that our films would not only be scary, but enjoyable and relatable; films that audiences would still want to watch thirty years from now.

Launching the site with *Soundbite* was the best idea, I feel, because it was such a simple and fun story about a young college girl who decides to listen to this new song she has heard about: Death Song - where supposedly, if you listen to the song, it will kill you. Surely, she was strong enough to listen to the song and not fall under its spell.... or is she?

Even better was doing a follow up with our film *Stalk*, including the silent killer type: an homage to *Halloween*, played by Tyler Gallant or *Love Me Not*, which was a fun exploration into online dating and the perils of breaking a young woman's heart.

I know these aren't stories of killers with knives who terrorize young adults in their sleep - but they are created with 'my voice,' and that is, albeit (in small way), a gift I get to give to the world. So, for the person who walked off their job at the age of 30 to follow their dream; I am reminded every day how grateful I am that I took that leap of faith.

I never knew that having a love of horror would push me to follow my passion and lead me onto a path of becoming a voice for those who need inspiration. I feel both honored and grateful to be on this path. Thank you, Wes Craven. Thank you, Robert Englund. Thank you, Freddy Kreuger!

THE EXORCIST
BY
EILEEN DIETZ

Actress
The Exorcist, Clownado, Lake Alice,
Helter Skelter, The Assent, Itsy Bitsy
Instagram: @EileenDietz Twitter: @QueenOfScreams
Facebook: @Eileen.Dietz

The Exorcist is my favorite horror movie for many reasons. It was the first major film I was cast in. I had shot a lot of projects before, from soap operas *The Doctors* and *Guiding Light* (both now extinct) to my first film *Teenage Gang Debs* (a drive in movie in B&W with an awesome soundtrack), and a PBS Special on various stages of pollution called *Foul*, starring Sam Waterston and Charlotte Rae. (My character was supposed to have a baby with Sam, but it turned out to be a huge chicken egg because we only ate chicken since beef was bad for us.) I also did a play called *Steambath* with Hector Elizondo as a Puerto Rican steam attendant at a bathhouse that was between Heaven and Hell. The other cast was Dick Shawn, Rip

Torn, and Charles Grodin, and it was directed by Tony Perkins
who eventually took over the lead, which he had wanted to do
from the beginning, but I digress.

I then did a Joyce Carol Oates play at a NY waiver theatre
called *Ontological Proof of My Existence.* Agents Fifi Oscard
and Martin Gage were in the audience, and they called me the
very next day to ask if I wanted to audition for a film called
The Exorcist. Fifi said they were looking for someone small and
strong who could act. I was strong, and had ridden horses since
I was 7, so I agreed. I went into the casting office of Marion
Dougherty and Juliet Taylor for the audition that would change
my life.

Juliet told me they were searching for a girl who could
look like a young actress named Linda Blair. Since the film was
being made from a book written by William Blatty, she asked
me to read it that night and come back in a few days to do
an improvisation from it. To say I was entranced, delighted,
and frightened by the book is an understatement. I finished it
that very night thinking, "How the hell do you play a demon?"
Aaaah! Wild animals came to mind. The next day, I went to
the public library and got a book on wild animals. That night, I
pulled down my shades, turned off the lights, lit some candles,
and started growling like a lion and yowling like a wolf. Satisfied, I went to bed dreaming of jungle beasts and demons

The next day, I got on the floor and played both parts.
"Mommy, mommy help me, help me!" I cried in a high-pitched
voice. "You sow! You pig!" I growled. Back and forth, I performed as a 12-year-old child and an ancient demon. It was
almost hypnotic. Juliet just sat there and said nothing. "Uh oh,"
I thought. Then she said, "Okay, that was great. Now, I want
you to meet the director and the makeup artist (who turned out
to be William Friedkin and the awesome makeup guru Dick
Smith), but maybe you should get a little smaller." That was
odd, because I was quite androgynous and lithe then. "Okay,"
I thought. I remembered magazines that sold plastic suits that
made you sweat. Well, I didn't have time for that, so I wrapped

myself in Saran Wrap and rode my bike for hours in Central Park. A few days later, I went to The Plaza Hotel, not only to meet Mr. Friedkin and Dick Smith, but Linda and her mom. That apparently worked out, because the next thing I knew, I was in Dick Smith's amazing studio a couple miles out of New York City, where I heard all of Dick's stories about working with the likes of Marlon Brando and Dustin Hoffman while he made a life mask of me to see if I could possess Regan in the movie. Next came the screen test where, again, I played both parts. The crew had a great sense of humor, brought me a three-foot crucifix for the scene, and I was cast.

All of this was a dream come true. Oh my God, I was in a major studio motion picture. I was about to work with Max Von Sydow (who I knew of from his Swedish Igmar Bergman films) and Jason Miller (author the Pulitzer-winning Broadway play, That Championship Season). On the first morning, I vividly remember sitting in the makeup chair as Dick applied prosthetics to make me look like the demon Pazuzu (who became known as Captain Howdy). I ended up acting in most of the controversial scenes in the film: I levitated, I vomited, I masturbated, and I did the death scene. I was brought up an atheist, but every day before we shot, I prayed to spirits, gods, and whomever to say, "Hey this is just a movie, this is just a part," just in case.

The shooting of *The Exorcist* became the talk of New York, filming on a huge soundstage on 54th Street between 9th and 10th Avenues. When I would walk into an office, a picture would fall down, and it was my fault. Strange things would happen and they would ascribe it to me.

I believe I was on the film for four months, with several weeks off while they rebuilt the entire living room set.

The makeup took 3-and-a-half hours to apply and an hour to take off (when all I really wanted to do was to go home). They turned televisions to face the mirrors so Linda and I could watch TV while they applied our makeup. Linda wanted to watch *I Love Lucy* at 7am, while I preferred the news. Oh well. I would often say "Good morning" to Dick's automaton dummy that caused Regan's head to turn around.

We kept wondering when the film would wrap and made bets on it, setting our birthdays as a stopping point. But it went on and on. Several of us had other offers, but we could not leave because this WAS *The Exorcist*.

On the very last day of production, we shot Captain Howdy, which became the demonic icon of the entire film. Warner Bros. uses it on all publicity, and it's even the face on the new soundtrack album. That old makeup test has made me famous in the tight-knit horror community.

When it wrapped, none of us thought it would become *THE EXORCIST*: THE SCARIEST MOVIE OF ALL TIME! Forty-five years later, people still tell me it is the scariest movie they have ever seen. When it came out, it was a mystery to the audience, since it was the first absolutely closed set where no one was allowed in: no journalists; no reporters; no one. When it was released, they wouldn't even let moviegoers in after the film started playing (also a first), so long, long lines waited outside the theatre for the next screening to begin. People fainted in the aisles, and some threw up as they ran outside to get away. They also did publicity stunts that had never been done before.

In the original version, the flashing face of Pazuzu was only seen once. Fans asked, "Did you see that?" "What?" "That face?" "What face?" And they went to see the film again just to my face! Of course there were no VCRs or DVDs then, so when the film was finally on TV, no one could pause it like they do now.

It was cinematic history...and I was part of it.

I must admit, I felt some pangs of guilt back then. Was I partly responsible for this terror? Was it a good thing or a bad thing? I did not know. Although there is so much real-life horror today with newscasts of war, mass murderers, and unspeakable acts of violence, I believe it is totally cathartic to teenagers, and especially young adults, to experience this kind of fear in film rather than than on the TV and in the news. Luckily, horror cinema has a beginning, middle, and end, unlike real life.

Ever since *The Exorcist*, I have gone on to shoot at least 20 horror films. As a matter of fact, all I do now is shoot horror and I am very happy about it. I love it!

Because of that film, I've been to the U.K., Germany and Spain (at Sitges Film Festival). I have been to 30 conventions in 30 states, answering questions about the film and hearing their stories about how seeing it ruined their childhoods (but they say it with a grin). They are as delighted to meet Captain Howdy as I am delighted to meet them. I think an obligation of film is to move people, make them feel things, perhaps learn things, but certainly take them on a cinematic ride, so they come out of the theatre saying, "WOW."

And like that, I say I am so proud to have been a tiny part of cinematic history.

DARK NIGHT OF THE SCARECROW

BY
RONNIE ANGEL

Author/Professional Wrestler
Slashed Dreams: The Ultimate Guide to Slasher Films, PETS,
Slashed Dreams Part 2: The Nightmare Continues
Runaway Nightmare, Meathook Massacre: The Final Chapter,
Frankie's Redemption, Tales from the Grave 2
Facebook: @Ronnie.Angel.18

It all started one dark and stormy night in 1990. A young me decided it would be fun to disregard my mother's orders to be in bed, while she watched the premiere of a little Stephen King film you may have heard of called *It*. I hid behind the couch as the show started and tried to be quiet. Well, as soon as the first scene unfolded where Pennywise attacks the little girl, I blew my cover. I remember screaming and running off down the hallway. Needless to say, I slept in my parent's room that night and was traumatized for a while afterwards.

Something strange happened after this though. I became incredibly fascinated by the horror section of Front Row Seat, my local video store in Farmington, New Mexico. I became entranced by the frightening box art and wondered what some of the films might be. My parents were pretty strict though, so I could only imagine the horrors that lurked in some of these boxes. Fast-forward a few years to when we moved to Sin City itself, Las Vegas, when my life was changed forever thanks to a late-night horror host named Count Cool Rider (today familiar to many fans as Korie Koker of the show *Counting Cars*).

It was during the Halloween season that I saw the advertisements for a special late night showing of the horror classic *Halloween*. I snuck downstairs when I was supposed to be in bed, turned the volume on low so I wouldn't wake anyone, and settled in. By the time it was over, I was forever changed. I had become a full-fledged horror addict. I would tune in to The Count every week, discovering classics such as *The Texas Chain Saw Massacre*, *Friday the 13th*, and so many more. I also started to discover some of the more obscure films thanks to shows like *USA Up All Night* and *Monstervision*. This was the dawn of what would become a lifelong love affair with horror. I would scour the horror section of every mom-and-pop video shop I came across, and I picked up back issues of *Fangoria* from the local comic book stores, discovering even more films to check out.

The funny thing about those mom-and-pop video shops is that the selection always varied from place to place. While one may have oddities like *Ants!* and *The Town That Dreaded Sundown*, the next shop might have neither, but have *Don't Go in The Woods* and *The Spookies*. Exploring was half the fun back then. I moved around a lot too, which gave me an opportunity to find new shops every place I went. We ended up in Durango, Colorado soon after, where I made the local Hesperus Video my new home. They had the most amazing selection in there, from *Highway to Hell* to *The Nailgun Massacre* (yeah, my mom loved that one). While scouring the shelves one day, there was a certain film that stood out to me. It didn't look like the others. It didn't have the intricate artwork that adorned most of the covers at the time. The picture on the cover looked cheap and grainy, simple really. It was just a picture, not artwork, of a sinister looking scarecrow on a cross, standing in the middle of the cornfield. That's it! Unfortunately for me, it was checked out, so I had to come back. A week later, the same bad news. The following week, the same. I came to discover that it had in fact been stolen and never returned. I searched high and low, but no other shops carried the title. Ordering it was also out of the question, as it was incredibly rare. Damn it, I was thwarted again!

As it turns out, luck was on my side. It came in quite the twisted way, though. I was kind of a bad kid while I was growing up. I used to steal cartons of cigarettes from the store and sell them at the junior high, one pack at a time. I became the pusher in some respects. Well, my new friends and I decided to make this Halloween a special one. We were going to have our first party and do it in style…in a graveyard! As luck would have it though, I got caught on this particular expedition. The time in the holding cell didn't bother me too much. Neither did the community service I had to endure after. No, what hurt the most was the fact that for the first time in my twelve years, I was grounded…on my favorite night of the year. That hurt. Fate has a weird way of working out though, as it turned out to be my favorite Halloween! I passed out candy, scared the crap out of younger kids, then proceeded to turn on the TV after the trick or treating died down. For the first time, I managed to watch the classic *Night of the Living Dead,* and became a lifelong Romero fan. The real surprise though, was finding out that following the zombie classic was none other than my long sought-after holy grail, *Dark Night of the Scarecrow*!! I was so excited. Finally, I was going to get to watch the film that I had been after for so long!

I settled in with a bowl of leftover candy as the eerie music played over the opening shots of the desolate midwestern corn-fields. By the time it was over, I was not disappointed one bit. It was everything I had ever hoped for and more. The story is about a special needs man in a small midwestern town named Bubba (played by the always entertaining Larry Drake), who is close friends with a little girl named Mary Lee. Of course, a group of local good ol' boys, led by the postman Mr. Hazelrigg (played by the legendary Charles Durning), don't take too kindly to this friendship and it seems odd to them, thus they have a history of tormenting the poor man. One day, Mary Lee is attacked by a dog, but Bubba comes to the rescue. The locals think that Bubba did it and set out to take him out. They eventually find Bubba hiding in a field, disguised as a scarecrow, hanging from a post. Before Bubba has any chance, the men execute Bubba with their own version of a firing squad. Just moments later, a call comes through the radio revealing Bubba not as an assailant, but a hero. The moment is haunting, as the early evening wind sets in, swaying Bubba's corpse as it hangs from the post.

The men claim self-defense and, after a lengthy trial, they are found not guilty. Both Mary Lee's mother and the district attorney warn that there are other means of justice out there. From there, all of the men start to meet their untimely ends. Most of them look like accidents, but Hazelrigg knows better. The other men keep seeing a scarecrow in their field before they meet their fate. It's believed that they're marked; that something supernatural is at work. Hazelrigg searches for any rational explanation, blaming anyone he can for it, and eventually spirals into a nervous wreck of a man, paranoid and dangerous. It all leads to an epic ending in the middle of a desolate field, where the scarecrow ultimately has his revenge.

Dark Night of the Scarecrow was legitimately eerie and suspenseful. The unnerving calm of the cornfields served as a perfect backdrop for this tale of vigilante justice gone wrong and the ever so satisfying revenge on the perpetrators. It was a suspenseful mystery and, to this day, the ending itself can be a bit of a head scratcher, adding to its mystique. It turned out to be the perfect Halloween seasonal film for when the nights get shorter and the air starts to get that little chill in it. With that one viewing, the film quickly became a new favorite of mine. The only problem? It was pretty rare to find a copy. Other than the much-cherished occasional October showing, there was no other way to see it. For years, I tried to find a copy, until I finally discovered one on eBay. Since then, it's become a regular watch. Eventually, it received a much-needed restoration and re-release on DVD and Blu-ray, introducing the film to new generations. Ever since, it's become a cult classic, and I couldn't be happier about it. It truly is much deserved.

After I began my foray into the horror business, I decided to get a tattoo from one of my favorite films to show my appreciation to the genre. It had to be one that was meaningful though, something that not everyone and their grandma has a tattoo of; something that was near and dear to me. I chose the image from *Dark Night of the Scarecrow* right after the kill shot, as a lifeless Bubba hangs from the post. That eerie moment serves as a precursor to the later hellish events of the film, where the atmosphere is so tense, it made the hair on my neck stand-up upon my first viewing. To this day, it's still my all-time favorite tattoo and the film still means the world to me. It reminds me of my favorite Halloween and the night I truly fell in love with horror. I've had the opportunity to speak with several of the people involved in the film (including the late Larry Drake) and they were all very appreciative of the dedication to the film, which is why this my favorite horror movie.

EVIL DEAD II
BY
ROBERT PARIGI

Writer/Director/Producer
Love Object, Tales from the Crypt,
Marvel's Agents of S.H.I.E.L.D.
Facebook: @Robert.Parigi

I saw my first horror movie so early that I don't even remember it. It has always been with me. If I could remember it, that would be my favorite. A family story says that one day, I was watching TV and told Mom, "Herman Munster isn't acting funny anymore." Maybe it was *House of Frankenstein*? Even before this, I must have already loved *The Munsters*. I suppose I was born this way. Decades later, my next most important horror movie experience is *Evil Dead II: Dead by Dawn*. It was on a double-bill with *Re-Animator*, which I had already seen, so for brevity's sake, I'll focus on *Evil Dead II*. It was a screening that changed my life forever...

I was getting a PhD in philosophy at SUNY Stony Brook, marking time until I transferred to Yale. Previously, I had escaped Beaumont, Texas with a scholarship to Trinity University in San Antonio. It had one of the best film schools in Texas, so I attended it to learn how to make horror movies. However, on the first day of class, Dr. Manfred von Wolfram declared, "Film is dead. Video is the future." He canceled the film program on the spot.

20 years later, Manfred might be right, but in the meantime, I had to study something to keep my scholarship. Philosophy had the same weirdness and imagination I loved in horror movies, and it became my new way of life. Like one of those dreams that seamlessly shifts to a distant location, I was suddenly in graduate school, getting a doctorate.

I was sitting in a small auditorium for the bargain matinee. The Chinese exchange students that used to give me rides to the multiplex were no longer speaking to me after I had convinced them to ditch Madonna's *Shanghai Surprise* for David Lynch's *Blue Velvet*, so I had to take the bus.

I hadn't seen a horror movie in a while and had missed *The Evil Dead*. I wasn't expecting much from a sequel to a movie I had never seen, so I was gobsmacked by *Evil Dead II*'s manic energy, frenzied camera, and spectacular gore.

Evil Dead II is my favorite in the series (the term "franchise" feels so mercenary). I love them all, but *The Evil Dead* feels like a movie that is trying to be scary, and is funny because it fails. The production values feel shabby without creating an atmosphere of immediacy like *Night of the Living Dead* or *Last House on the Left*. *Army of Darkness* abandons horror altogether for all-out comedy and sword and sorcery fantasy. *Evil Dead II*, on the other hand, is a fully realized balance of effective horror and intentional comedy.

This time, the frenzied camera dances inside accomplished settings, with incredible creatures by KNB. Evil Ed's extra rows of teeth are a creepy detail; the mesmerizer lens POV along bending angles inside the cabin is still the most convincing evocation of an alien presence trying to force its way into our world; and overt violations of time and space, like the impossible sunset that traps Ash, are genuinely disturbing. Meanwhile, Bruce Campbell's Ash is one of the all-time great comic characters, ramping up Bob Hope's cowardly hero shtick for a splatstick universe. Surrounded as he is by supernatural horrors, we can sympathize with Ash's cowardice instead of holding it against him. Trapped in an illogical world of unknown rules and powers, we can identify with his stupidity. And yet, Ash eventually rises to the occasion. If he can't defeat the horror, he can at least blow it a raspberry.

Other touches are wonderfully odd: the monkey screeches when Henrietta's neck stretches, and the gasbag wheezes when her bloated, decapitated body collapses. The scene with Ash twitching in the chair, torn between a paralyzing fear to move and a panic to flee, is genuinely frightening, funny, and even tragic.

Seeing *Evil Dead II* was mind-expanding. More importantly, it was soul-expanding. For the first time in a long time, I was having fun! The wonder and weirdness that had attracted me to philosophy was absent from graduate school. I had forgotten the daemonic joy of horror. *Evil Dead II* reminded me. It was intoxicating.

Before I could crash from *Evil Dead II*, it was time for *Re-Animator*. I can't remember if it was a legitimate double feature, or if I sneaked into an adjacent screen.

Maybe it was the shock of randomly seeing two full-tilt, genre-busting classics back-to-back on the same day that provoked what happened next. I broke out in a cold sweat. I was overwhelmed with existential horror. Like some kind of near-death experience, my entire life streamed before my eyes…

-I remember visiting granddaddy Ging-Ging in Dallas one summer and seeing a shopping mall for the first time. My parents tell me I can pick out a toy. I pick a square-box Aurora Frankenstein model with glow-in-the-dark parts. My parents try to explain that it's not a toy, it has to be put together, and I can't even play with it. It will break. But I insist. I remember opening the box on the drive home to Beaumont, marveling at the beautiful, marble-like grey plastic, and the glow-in-the-dark head and hands like alabaster (before I know what that is). Even more vividly, I remember coming home from kindergarten and finding that Mom has built the kit for me. The marble and alabaster Frankenstein reminds me of the statues in St Ann's Catholic Church. I never break it. I still have it, Mom's paint job intact.

-Next I see myself seeing *King Kong* (1933). Dad takes me to a screening at Lamar University, where he is Professor of Economics. The screen is gigantic, in a huge amphitheater. In high school, I revisit the campus theater. It is small, the seats only slightly raked. Smaller even than the theatre in which I've just watched *Evil Dead II* and *Re-Animator*.

-I'm swept back into the memories. Everything flows to the cover of *Famous Monsters of Filmland Magazine* #94. It has a monochromatic San Julian cover painting of Karloff from *Bride of Frankenstein*. I won't discover Basil Gogos' psychedelic portraits until issue #99. For now, it is 1972. I see *FM* #94 in the magazine section at Mr. Brown's 7-11, on my way to the spinner rack for comic books. It is an epiphany. The old world falls away. *FM* #94 becomes the portal to a new world. It feels like home. Every issue is a capsule history of horror, from Meliés quaint pantomimes to modern terrors. My skin crawls as turning pages bring me closer to that "Mystery Photo" of the ghoul from *Night of the Living Dead*. I skip the whole issue featuring *The Exorcist* until I can handle it as a back-issue. Forry Ackerman's retrospective format shows a horror history full of changes, and therefore a future of evolving possibilities. I want to become part of those changes and that future.

-The Captain Company mail order ads are equally fascinating evidence of an entire horror culture. I get a paper route just so I can buy 8mm abbreviations of Universal horror classics and *FM* back issues. I watch the jittery clips from *House of Frankenstein* over and over, wondering if this is the movie I saw in the family story. I still don't know. Most fascinating are the Don Post Studios monster masks. "Made in North Hollywood, California!" The Fun Shop and Spencer Gift masks at Parkdale Mall are shabby by comparison. It takes a while to save up for my first Don Post, a Lon Chaney Wolf Man. I still have the mask, although the matching hands have rotted away from use.

-I surround myself with as many of these artifacts as I can, imaginary connections to my finally-remembered home planet. I want to help preserve our sacred relics for future generations, so I send a twenty-five dollar money order to the Ackerman Archives, aka the Ackermansion. Easter Sunday morning, as Mom and Dad are wrangling my older siblings and me for mass, I get a long-distance phone call from Los Angeles. It's Forrest J Ackerman, keeper of the Ackerman Archives, editor of *Famous Monsters*! He tells me, "Happy Easter to a good egg!"

-Soon after, my parents take me to Lamar one night to see Vincent Price on his 1970s lecture tour, "The Villain Still Pursues Me." I get to ask him a question from the audience about *The Invisible Man Returns*. He signs my copy of FM #94 and inspires my love of modern art.

-Meanwhile, Mr. Brown informs Mom that I have been buying "those" *Famous Monsters Magazines*. Did I have her permission? Although my parents never understood my interest in horror, they knew it was important to me. Mom says it's fine, and I never have any trouble at the store. I only learn about this conversation years later, when Mr. Brown dies and the store has a new owner.

-Now, I'm up until 2am on a school night to catch *Invasion of the Body Snatchers* on TV, before the advent of VCRs, DVDs, or VOD. Trying to stay awake becomes an eerily immersive experience. If you fall asleep, you'll turn into a pod person. Whatever you do, don't fall asleep!

-For now, I'm making horror movies to get out of writing school reports. *Earthquack* stars that Wolf Man mask and a new Don Post tentacle-faced Alien. A crazed seismologist studies animals' ability to anticipate earthquakes, especially a captive Wolf Man. An *Invaders* flying saucer model kit shoots scratched-out rays that cause an earthquake so big, the seismograph needle flies off the machine and impales the scientist, spraying blood. The Wolf Man escapes from the lab, just in time to fight the alien from the saucer. I play both parts, since I don't want anyone to ruin the masks. Firecrackers blow up the miniature dam, weakened by the alien's earthquake ray. Presumably, the flood wipes out the Wolf Man and Alien, but I never figure out how to get that shot. I get an A anyway.

-High school, VHS, and more super 8 movies follow. Teachers are still falling for that gag. Suckers. In *American Inventors and Inventions*, I'm the narrator who accidentally grinds off his arm with Eli Whitney's cotton gin, electrocutes himself with Edison's light bulb, and spills acid on his face, reenacting Alexander Graham Bell's first phone call. Deranged by the mutilations, I pull off my bandages to reveal the surgical horrors of the Don Post Studios Frankenstein 2001 mask, and attack the camera with my hook hand. I still have that mask, and that plastic pirate hook.

-Working as a ticket taker and then a projectionist at the UA Phelan 6, I always time my breaks with free nachos and Dr. Pepper to watch Eddie Quist's transformation in *The Howling* and Norris' heart attack in *The Thing*, or the tenement raid in *Dawn of the Dead* and dinner party in *The Texas Chain Saw Massacre* on their Dollar Night Tuesday re-releases. I get to keep all the 1980s slasher one sheets because no one else wants them.

All of this washes over me in an icy torrent in that Long Island multiplex not unlike the one where I worked in high school a few years before. I shudder awake: I'm Cesare, suddenly waking up from Dr. Caligari's trance and finding myself on crazy, tilting rooftops. I teeter on the brink of the void, dizzy and nauseous, and break out in a cold sweat like Talking Head's "Once in a Lifetime." My God! What have I done?! Why am I in graduate school? Whatever happened to making horror movies?!

Existential crisis or panic attack? Whatever it is, it's the exact opposite of my *Famous Monsters* epiphany. Instead of a new world opening up, I see it spiraling away, like the tunnel Ash opens up with the Necronomicon. I have to get back inside, before it's gone forever!

Evil Dead II and *Re-Animator* saved me. They woke me up just in time: a bit longer, and I would have become a pod person. My entire professional life in horror begins with that screening.

I threw away the transfer scholarship to Yale to pound the pavement in NYC, desperately trying to pry my way into movie-making like the exiled Deadites squirming through dimensional angles in Ash's cabin. Just as the annoyed receptionist at New Line Cinema was about to throw me out, a guy in the shipping department reminds her that Mike DeLuca is looking for script readers. I luck into a job writing freelance coverage, learning more than in any screenwriting class.

Freelance reading at New Line in New York leads to a set P.A. gig on one of their movies shooting in Los Angeles, which rolls into another P.A. gig on the *Freddy's Nightmares* TV series, shooting in the North Hollywood warehouse behind us. Finally, I'm working on horror!

Oddly enough, another warehouse down the street was Don Post Studios. I remember the tags on my masks: "Made in North Hollywood, California!" One of the first directors I meet on *Freddy's Nightmares* is William Malone, one of the Masters of Horror. An all-around horror artist and filmmaker, Bill sculpted The Shape's mask in *Halloween*, and also that Wolf Man mask, the tentacle-faced Alien, Frankenstein 2001, and even the Thanatoid mask I bought from a dusty Times Square novelty shop to remind me of my newly-recovered vocation. In 2013, I helped re-issue Thanatoid with Trick Or Treat Studios. Now one of my closest friends, Bill sculpted an update of Frankenstein 2001 to replace my decaying original copy.

String enough gigs together, and eventually you have a career. For me, it all started with that double feature of *Evil Dead II* and *Re-Animator*. So tonight my favorite horror movie is *Evil Dead II*. Tomorrow, it might be *Re-Animator*, or *Cabinet of Dr. Caligari*, or *Rosemary's Baby*, or *Dawn of the Dead*, or *Bride of Frankenstein*, or *Eraserhead*, or....

LADY IN WHITE
BY
AARON LAPLANTE

Voice Actor/Writer/Artist
Primal, Samurai Jack,
Hotel Transylvania 3, B`aki, Naruto
Instagram: @Dooder3

B eing asked to write a piece for the next volume of a
book called *My Favorite Horror Movie* is the only way I
could ever force myself to pick a favorite. My enthusiasm for horror knows no bounds. Like many horror fans, I
don't care what the story is, just so long as it has a ghost, a
monster, a murderer, or better yet, all three. That doesn't help
when trying to narrow it down. So after many sleepless nights
and some intense soul searching, I would like to say officially,
and in writing, that my favorite horror movie is: *The Lady in
White* by Frank LaLoggia.

Whether you've seen it or not, the movie has an honored
place in the illustrious tradition of what I like to call "secret
handshake" movies. It's not a franchise. There were no action

figures, no appearances on any top ten lists (that I'm aware of), and you can't pay 20 dollars at a horror convention for the autograph of a person who got killed in it. It's just a classic ghost story with everything a true horror fan could ever want: ghosts, murderers, mystery, and an amazing score. I don't come across too many people who have seen it, but when I do, we feel like members of a secret society.

Over the years, I've pitched this movie more times than I can count. I've talked about it on podcasts, at horror conventions, to new friends, old friends, and basically anyone who will listen. I'm a self ordained minister in the gospel of *The Lady In White*, and I preach the good word any chance I get. The pitch usually goes something like this:

> "HOLY SHIT, you haven't seen *Lady In White*? Really? Oh you have to see it. I've got a couple copies. I will lend you one. In fact, you can just keep it. You're gonna want to keep it. Are you sure you don't remember? On the VHS cover there was a little kid with a terrified look on his face and a Halloween mask pulled up over his head crouching next to a window with the moonlight shining through. No?
>
> It's just a great classic ghost story with a lot of heart, and it's legitimately spooky. The movie is kind of like *Stand By Me* in that it's an incredibly nostalgic coming of age story that was made in the eighties but takes place around the late fifties or early sixties. It has a very '80s vibe but not in a *Sixteen Candles* kind of way, in a "children coming of age through intense danger" kind of way.
>
> The story focuses on a young boy who gets locked in the cloakroom of his school by some bullies on Halloween night. While sitting in the darkness, he hears the sound of a child laughing. Now if that wasn't terrifying enough, the appa-

rition of a little girl floats through the locked cloakroom door and talks to someone who isn't there. At first, the little girl is happy, singing and dancing around the room, but soon after, something scares her. She pleads to go home and wants her mommy. The boy watches in horror as an invisible figure strangles the screaming girl to death, then carries her lifeless body out of the room. Before the boy can even process what he just saw, the door to the cloakroom bursts open and man with a flashlight enters. We can't see his face in the darkness and neither can the boy. It's clear that this is not help arriving to save him. The boy stays quiet as the man searches around the room trying to find something. When the man notices that that he's not alone in the room, the boy pulls his Halloween mask over his face so as not to be seen. Suddenly, the man grabs the boy, choking him violently. As the boy closes his eyes, we see a montage of thoughts going through his head. Everything cuts to black. The boy wakes up surrounded by police and his father giving him CPR.

And that's only the beginning! So basically from this point on, it's a hybrid ghost story and murder mystery. For the rest of the movie, the boy has to find out who the little girl is as well as who tried to kill him. Its awesome and you will love it!!!!!!!!"

Okay maybe the pitch is not THAT in-depth but I have to pique the interest of the uninitiated. After all, I'm not talking someone's ear off at a horror convention. This is being written in a book that's going to be published. This is my chance to spread the word on a larger scale!

Despite my rabid enthusiasm for the movie, I do understand its slight obscurity. It seems to have suffered the same fate as a lot of movies in the eighties. The decade was a particularly fertile time for what I like to call "children in peril" movies where the kids are the heroes, forced to come of age in the face of dangerous and sometimes supernatural circumstances. These movies were confusing for the paying audiences. *Are they kids movies for grown-ups or grown-up movies for kids?* As a result, these movies spent little to no time in the theaters, only to be put on VHS in a time when video stores only carried one copy of each movie and they were quite easy to miss. To paraphrase a quote from the great Dana Gould, "When I was a kid, seeing a movie was like seeing a deer."

I did discover it on VHS, but not at my local video store. It was one of several movies that my dad taped while using a cable box to steal Showtime. (I don't know if the statute of limitations has run out on stealing Showtime, but I would love to see them try to go after my dad, he's a tough old bastard.) It was not the first horror movie I saw but it was the first one that I saw myself in. The main character was about my age, the story took place in a small town similar to mine, and the family dynamic of the characters was familiar to me. It scared me half to death when I first watched it. My brother fondly recalls watching me jump across the living room to get away from the TV at one point. I can easily mark that moment as my birth into horror fandom. I didn't go screaming out of the room, though. Instead, I giggled a little bit, pulled myself together, and sat back down to finish the movie. It was in that moment that I embraced the concept of being entertained by being scared.

While *The Lady In White* was my gateway drug into the world of horror, it was not the horrific elements that resonated with me the most. In addition to creating the perfect blend of creepiness and nostalgic sentiment, I could tell that the story was intensely personal to the filmmaker. I didn't need any special features or commentary to see that. The characters are not just arbitrary victims and villains, they are universally relatable and at the same time, incredibly specific. They came from somewhere - certainly the creativity of the writer, but I have the feeling that it also came from his own life experience. I didn't know it at the time, but the movie pressed a subconscious button in me that I didn't even know existed. It set a precedent for how I want stories to be told and how I want to tell them myself. The most basic and common writing advice anyone gets is, "Write what you know". Personally, I always had a hard time accepting that. My self-esteem would get in the way of me thinking that anyone would ever care to know my experience, let alone read a script about it. I became free of that self-doubt once I realized that they don't mean write EXACTLY what you know. Embellish. A detailed account of me eating a sandwich by myself in my car while parked in the Hollywood Forever Cemetery is not that interesting, but if halfway through the story I looked up from wiping a fallen glob of mayonnaise off my shirt and noticed a hand coming up out of a grave, that would be a story worth telling. A vivid and relatable reality stems from something personal and perfectly sets the stage for an entertaining story. Frank LaLoggia's writing taught me that.

There has not been much written about the movie. You can't find too many interviews with Frank LaLoggia talking about his own personal experience and how it might have influenced *The Lady In White,* so I could only speculate on the personal nature of the story. It wasn't until I actually contacted Frank himself that I got an indication.

I found the writer/director (on Facebook of all places) and saw that he was living in Italy. I took a shot in the dark and wrote him a long and probably incoherent message about his movie and what it means to me. Amazingly, he wrote me back. We continued corresponding after that, just checking in and saying hi. He was very gracious in letting me gush about his movie and I think he genuinely appreciated it. After a few months, I got the courage up to send him a few things that I had made. One was a comedy short that I wrote and directed and was based on something very personal that I had been dealing with. The other was a horror-comedy short that I acted in, but was written and directed by a friend of mine. I was a bit embarrassed by the one I wrote. It was the first time I'd ever written and directed anything, and the technical quality was a bit rough. The horror short on the other hand, was incredibly well made, a great script, amazing special effects, and just wildly entertaining. I thought for sure Frank would love it. As it turned out, he didn't love it. In fact his actual words on the horror short were, "It's technically proficient but I just didn't give a fuck". You can imagine my deflation at reading this. But then he went on to say how much he enjoyed the short that I had written and directed. He said that it made him laugh and that he could relate to it. He could tell that it came from a real place emotionally. So there you have it, the person who single-handedly inspired my entire taste for and approach to storytelling confirmed my speculation and gave me his blessing. What could be better?

If you're one of the many who hasn't seen the *Lady in White*, please do yourself a favor and watch it. Then after you're done watching, please immediately show it to someone else who hasn't seen it, preferably a kid. If they're lucky, the movie will do for them what it did for me. It truly has the power to jumpstart a lifetime of enjoyment in the horror genre. Every horror fan will agree: to be a horror fan is to be lucky. We have the distinct privilege of loving and being excited by what scares everyone else. It's a fun life.

Oh, and by the way, I know I've spent this whole time talking it up, but if you aren't a horror fan, you might not like this movie. The special effects, though state of the art at the time, are rather cheesy by today's standards. But…if you aren't a horror fan, why the hell are you reading this book?

THE TINGLER
BY
MYK WATFORD

Actor/Musician
*The Kitchen, True Detective, Trailer Park of Terror, No Country
For Old Men, Law & Order SVU, Breaking Bad*
Instagram: @Myk_Watford Twitter: @MykWatford
Facebook: @MykWatfordFans MykWatford.com

North Georgia, late 1970s. We lived in an area called Clock Tower Hill in Rome. It was, and still is, one of the oldest neighborhoods in North Georgia, with post-Civil War homes built by aspiring, young, upper-middle class southern families after Sherman had burned most of the town to the ground on his March to the Sea. But you wouldn't find any of these homes on the historic registry. Not then anyway. It was a forgotten neighborhood. Nearly 150 years ago, it was brimming with promise, but most of that promise had moved on. Now, it was just an assemblage of very old houses in a very old neighborhood on a very high hill. Every hour, the old bronze bell from 1872 still rang, almost as a death knell to the ramshackle streets it loomed over.

Our little piece of this vicinage was a three bedroom crafts-man, which, to a seven year old boy, seemed to have walls that went clear up to the sky. It was a noisy old place with dark cor-ners and crooked floors - not much of a yard for a boy to play in being planted on such a high hill. Our entertainment was movies, predominantly old movies, and usually B level horror classics. This was not my choice, per se. My mother was a hor-ror movie nut, and until we got HBO a couple years later, it was usually pretty much whatever pot-boiling black & white chiller that came through the bunny ears. She viewed it as a duty of sorts: to christen my sister and I in these forms of entertain-ment. I suppose she thought it would toughen us up a little, but mostly, I think, she wanted us to understand and appreciate the form and art itself. Whether it accomplished any of this, I cannot say. What I can say is that I have a vivid recall of al-most every scary old movie we watched in that old house...and perhaps, none more dramatic than the first...the 1959 William Castle classic *The Tingler*, starring Vincent Price.

So there we were, my sister and I, propped up on our el-bows on the old afghan rug, as my mom sat behind us on the couch. We had no idea what we were in for. At least I didn't.

It didn't take long for the movie to put me on edge. At the top of the film, William Castle himself appears on screen to warn the audience that the things happening to the charac-ters in the movie are very real and that some of those watch-ing will experience the same, terrifying phenomena depicted in the film. I wasn't sure where this was going, but it was very unsettling. Castle went on to plead that anyone experiencing overwhelming fear while viewing the picture must immediate-ly scream, adding, "Remember, if you scream at just the right time, it just might save your life."

To this day, I have never seen another director appear pre-screening to inform the audience that his film might lit-erally scare them to death. This warning landed severely and legitimately inside my seven-year-old mind. I might actually die watching this movie…wait…what?

I looked back to my mother. "If you get sacred, just scream," she said, concerned. I made a mental note, clinching the afghan rug into balls in my fist. It sure didn't help that our old house creaked and groaned like a decaying old man every time the wind blew.

There were parts of the movie that seemed old fashioned and dated; others that were wildly effective and genuinely terrifying, like when a deaf mute, unable to articulate her fear, is spun into madness upon seeing a hand rise from a pool of deep crimson blood in her bathtub (incidentally, the only part of the movie that was colorized - the blood). She ultimately collapsed and died of sheer panic, a victim of "The Tingler," according to Vincent Price.

My heart raced. I looked around to see my mother's reaction. Asleep. My sister? Out like a light. I froze. It was just me and Vincent Price now. "It's just an old movie…it isn't real," I told myself.

But that premise unnerved me, looming in my brain like that old clock on the hill. I couldn't stop thinking about it and the director's ominous warning; "If you scream at just the right time, it just might save your life." It must be true if he was forced to say something like that for the good of everyone watching. Yes, it must certainly be real. I gulped, preparing my parched throat for what may inevitably come. Best be ready. "I am too young to die," I thought.

But what was it? The Tingler? Vincent Price was certainly hell-bent on finding out, and now I had to know, too.

It didn't take long.

I watched in horror as Vincent Price, backlit behind a white curtain, cut into this poor dead woman's spine, and the shadow of a giant insect-like creature emerged from it. It was long and floppy with many tiny little arms, like a giant nightmarish centipede.

Could this be true? The Tingler was a real, living thing? A creature that dwells within us, feeding off our fears? I went flush. A moment of deep realization: that feeling we have, that I had at that very moment, when terror shivers up our spine... was a living organism. And if we did not, or could not, express our fears, it would grow and grow, until it would finally literally crack our spine in two.

Trapped inside my own anxiety, I was beginning to feel a bit like this poor old dead deaf mute lady. Should I scream right here and now? Just get it out of the way to be safe? I cleared my throat just in case.

The wind howled, the old floor grumbled, and Tingler got loose in a theater of unsuspecting moviegoers. Thankfully, Vincent Price captured the creature and was ultimately able to destroy it by placing it back in the body of the dead deaf mute lady, a place where it cold no longer cause harm or fear.

Thank god. I made it through and I didn't even scream. I sighed with relief. "It was just an old movie," I laughed. How silly of me to have even considered it to be real.

What the hell time was it, anyway? Almost midnight. Way too late for a second grader to be up watching scary movies. I reached over to turn the television off...but something strange happened. The screen went black. And then...a voice. Vincent Price's ghoulish tenor crackles through the speaker. "Ladies and gentlemen, a word of warning; If any of you are not convinced that you have a tingler of your own, the next time you are afraid in the dark...don't scream." Was he talking to me? I flinched, reflexively turning the TV off.

And now, not 2 seconds after Vincent Price had uttered those words, I stood there in a very dark room, very afraid. I began to feel my blood run slowly cold and the hair on my neck stand up. My heart thumped and my back shivered. SHIVERED? Oh no. Is that it? Is that The Tingler? I felt as if I might faint. Suddenly, there was a loud noise. A deafening crashing that rang in my ears and reverberated my brain. "This is it!" I thought, "This is the Tingler!" I felt a panic setting in. Clang!...Clang!...Clang! I had to do something. I had to scream! I opened my mouth wide and readied myself to unleash a thunderous holler, the likes of which would surely wake every peanut farmer in Floyd County. But just before the scream escaped my trembling lips, there was another voice...this time, my mother's. "The bell," she groaned. I turned to her...her eyes half open. The bell? She pointed up the hill. Of course. The old bell in the clock tower. Whew...my clenched shoulders slowly rolled back into place. I looked around, getting my bearings. Everything was fine. I wasn't going to die after all.

"Go to bed, son," she yawned.

As I lay there in bed, eyes wide open, my mother peeked in. "Goodnight son...I love you...and there's no such thing as The Tingler." She stepped away, then slowly leaned back in as the old floor creaked. "But to be safe...if you get scared...just scream..."

ROSEMARY'S BABY
BY
NAJARRA TOWNSEND

Actress
Contracted, Wolf Mother, Me and You and Everyone We Know
Najarra.com
Instagram: @Najarra

Growing up, I didn't think I was a big fan of horror movies. I didn't like the feeling of being on edge; the discomfort that comes with suspense and the fact that scary movies would linger with me for days, weeks, and sometimes years later. But I always did find myself drawn to them. The adrenaline rush that came with the fear was addictive. I was the kid who would agree to see a horror movie and then keep my hands over my eyes for most of it.

The first movie I remember being truly frightened by was *Fire in the Sky* (specifically that alien probing scene). Although it is labeled a sci-fi movie, it terrified me, staying with me into adulthood, creating a fear and fascination with aliens. I always found that the kind of films I enjoyed the most were the ones that felt based in reality and were psychologically taxing; *The Silence of the Lambs, The Shining, The Sixth Sense, Candyman.* All of these horror films (and a few more) were the ones that created long-lasting fears within me.

When I was 10 years old, I booked my first feature film. It was a horror movie. Making that film at a young age did two things for me. One, it gave me the ability (after the fact) to watch a scary movie without going into it being afraid because I was able to take a step back and think "how did they make this?" And two: it made my appreciation for the horror genre much greater. You could take any subject matter and make a horror film about it. It is a genre that has every other genre within it. Plus, making a horror film is the ultimate fun. Letting your emotions run wild with all the usual crying and screaming is such a release; but going through makeup and prosthetics is one of the most exciting experiences; seeing how they make cuts, broken bones, gunshot wounds and heads explode; not to mention stunts! I've done things I never knew my body was capable of. It's truly magic in the making. I would continue, whilst growing up and throughout my career, to revisit horror and remind myself how much I loved making these kinds of films.

In 2012 I was cast in a film called *Contracted.* I was so excited to play the lead role of Samantha because it took me back to the kind of horror film I really loved. Although labeled a body horror (and not psychological), I was getting the chance to play a woman who feels like she's losing her mind. The chance to explore her mental breakdown made me so excited; to understand how one can be in such great denial that they can't see what's really going on around and within them. The experience of filming *Contracted* was one of my most loved to date.

During the press for the release of the film, I was asked repeatedly what my favorite horror movie was. Now, I've never been one to have a favorite anything; I love options. But I had to have an answer so I took time to reflect on what horror movies could honestly be my actual favorite.

At first I thought it must be *The Shining*. Stanley Kubrick. Jack Nicholson. My forever fear of hotels. It's a classic! But saying that to people over time didn't feel true. I love that film, but it's just not my favorite. Then I decided it must be *A Nightmare on Elm Street*. The idea of not being able to go to sleep because you could die in your nightmares was truly terrifying and resonated with me (plus, Freddie Krueger is a legend). That song "One, Two, Freddie's coming for you" always gives me chills. But again, after a little while, I just wasn't sure anymore.

This went on for some time, but I always seemed to come back to one movie. A classic I first saw when I was a kid: *Rosemary's Baby*. At a young age, I knew I really liked the movie. Even though it didn't terrify me with jump scares and blood or gore, it left me with an eerie and unsettling feeling. I would find myself randomly thinking about it. The idea that evil can be in anyone, in your neighbour, your doctor, or even in your own bed.

For me, *Rosemary's Baby* is a film that has gotten scarier with age. And what makes a better psychological horror movie than one that keeps getting more frightening the older you get and the more you pay attention to the world? Over the years, I saw it a few more times and I loved it more and more with each viewing. I found myself continuously discovering new depths to my fears through watching it. Every time I finished a viewing, I was left mulling over some new bit I hadn't focused on previously. It is a film that always leaves me thinking; a film that plays on such visceral fears: being betrayed by the one you love the most and the people around you; the horrifying and real fact that evil people look just like normal people; the idea that all of your instincts are saying something is wrong but everyone around you makes you out to be crazy. And this is just the first few layers. I also love how much is left to your imagination. Throughout the entire film, there's only one shot of the devil, and in that single shot, they only reveal his eyes. You know when you're on a rollercoaster and you can feel your stomach fall out of your body on that first drop? That's what

I feel every time that shot of his eyes comes up in the film. I've always believed leaving some of the horror up to one's own imagination can be much more terrifying. It makes it so much more personal to what an individual finds scary.

As I recently sat down to watch the film, there was a new issue, a giant fear that I had never realized was so blatantly all over the movie. The right to your own body. Rosemary has no control over her own body. She is persuaded to think she does, but she is simply being manipulated and used as a vessel. What is more terrifying than having your freedom of choice taken away from you?

I have come to realize, partly through the process of writing this, that *Rosemary's Baby* is so much more than just my favorite horror movie. For me, this movie hits all the marks: witches, the '60s, gender dynamics, Mia Farrow, betrayal, women's rights, questioning your sanity, the desire to be a mom, Ruth Gordon, a beautiful, historic building, and even an eerie "la la" song. This is a film I will revisit throughout my life. A film I will continue to discuss and think about. A film that I can honestly say is my favorite horror movie.

I can now see why I was drawn to horror as a kid. These movies would linger with me, making me think about what I was afraid of; teaching me about my fears. They also taught me, in most cases, how to overcome my fears. I've learned a lot by watching horror films and having the privilege of being in them. I've grown up to become a huge horror fan, and I can proudly say I no longer watch horror movies with my hands over my eyes...most of the time.

VIDEODROME
BY
PRESTON FASSEL

Author/Journalist/Screenwriter/Creative Executive
Our Lady of the Inferno, Fangoria Magazine,
Rue Morgue, Screem, Cinedump
Twitter: @PrestonFassel

When I rented *Videodrome* from the Hollywood Video in Broken Arrow, Oklahoma, in the Summer of 2004, I had little idea of the sort of connection I would make with it, or the impact it would have on my life.

To say that I rented it accidentally wouldn't be quite accurate, although I also didn't pick it up with any intention of seeing the complete canon of David Cronenberg, or expanding my '80s horror education, or even watching a movie with Debbie Harry in it, although I was in the throes of a serious Blondie obsession. Rather, I picked it up as part of an ongoing quest to rent and watch every single movie in Hollywood Video's "Cult" section—a mysterious shelf tucked away in the back of the store that served as a catchall for films that either defied categorization or which couldn't comfortably be placed into one single genre without offending casual fans. This was where controversial but seminal works like *A Clockwork Orange* rubbed shoulders with grindhouse abominations like *Poor Pretty Eddie*; where obscure Aussie cinema sat alongside the films of John Waters. If a movie was compelling enough to carry, but too offensive, strange, or indescribable to stick anywhere else, you'd find it in the Cult Section; and the Cult Section is where I spent the bulk of that summer, slowly working my way down the list.

It was a quest that'd begun innocently enough when I decided to rent *Blue Velvet*, if "innocent" is ever an adjective that can be applied when David Lynch is involved. As a tween, my parents had gotten me a subscription to Johnson Smith's *Things you Never Knew Existed*, a novelties catalog that carried everything from magic tricks to kitschy home décor to obscure VHSes, which, in the early '90s, were inaccessible to most consumers outside of back alleys or the gray market. While I was initially drawn in by their sci-fi junk like *Star Trek* models and boxing alien hand puppets (don't ask), as a burgeoning horror fan, it was the movies that really grabbed by attention, especially as I hit my teens and the subversive and forbidden became more enticing and alluring. This was where I first learned of—and became fascinated by—*Freaks*, the film so shocking that it'd been "BANNED IN 20 COUNTRIES!" It was where I developed my lifelong crush on Elvira, Mistress of the Dark, the goth goddess billed as "THE ONE SPECIAL EFFECT STEVEN SPIELBERG CAN'T MATCH." It was where I became obsessed with one day seeing *Blue Velvet*, "THE MOVIE SO DISTURBING THEY DON'T WANT YOU TO SEE IT!" God bless the Johnson Smith folks; their ad copy sat at the perfect intersection of hyperbole and the honest truth, and it played a tremendous role in turning me into the sort of horror fan who isn't happy unless he's seeking out the next great obscure treasure.

So when I turned 17 in the fall of 2002, and had both the access and ability to rent *Blue Velvet*, I went ahead and rented it, eager to see what had been a forbidden secret to me for so many years. Would it live up to my expectations?

Yes, it would. To say that seeing *Blue Velvet* at 17 was a revelation for me is a tremendous understatement. I had no idea that films like this could exist and, seeing the VHS box sitting there in the Cult section, surrounded by dozens of other films, the idea that there could be more movies like it right at my fingertips was like being handed the keys to a Ferrari and told to have fun. Thus, it was then the great Cult Section Crusade of 2002-2004 began. Every Friday, like clockwork, I was there at the back of Hollywood Video. There was no formal plan of attack—I was a teenager, after all. Researching the individual movies and then renting them based on interest never occurred to me; nor did the alphabetical approach. In time-honored teenage tradition, I'd show up, head to the cult section, and rent whatever happened to look cool on a given night. Sometimes the criteria was more stringent—the movie that looked coolest might be rented out, so I'd have to rent whatever looked second coolest—but for the most part, I hacked my way through the section in no order whatsoever. Thus, it was that one night fifteen years ago, I found myself coming home with *Videodrome*.

I don't remember much about the actual watching experience—it was my introduction to David Cronenberg, so, understandably, I was a bit mind-blown by the time I hit rewind. I do remember though, being hit by a profound revelation the next day. By this point in my horror education, I'd seen countless movies I enjoyed; a few more that I genuinely loved. Videodrome, though, was the first horror movie I'd seen that I felt got me—and which I got in return.

As some of the dates I've given here indicate, I'm a child of the late '80s and early '90s. Though I properly came of age during the Bush-Clinton years, my memory is sharp enough—and I'm just old enough—to have experienced and remember some touchstone moments of the Reagan era. I watched the Berlin Wall come down on TV. I participated in a duck-and-cover drill. I saw A-Ha's "Take on Me" video on MTV back when MTV still played music videos. Too, my dad was an engineer for Southwestern Bell who occasionally brought his work home, meaning I was among the first generation of kids to be exposed to such things as "DOS" and "floppy discs" and this green, glowing thing called a "personal computer." In other words, I remember very well when the world looked like Videodrome, and watching it as a nominally friendless, confused teenager in the 9/11 era, I experienced a weird sort of comfort I hadn't felt for a long time. As strange as it may sound, *Videodrome* became something of a safe place for me—this world of daytime talk shows and glass block walls and clandestine video pirate labs was one into which I could escape, and remember an era before the crippling forces of adolescence and puberty hit me with a cruel double whammy. For a nostalgia trip, *The Breakfast Club* is too polished and *The Goonies* too whimsical, but my dad worked with guys who looked like Harlan, and I remember some of that technology, those glass block walls, and the beautiful, lost world of late-night television.

Also, the film's subject matter dovetailed with a number of my own interests, ones I wasn't used to seeing depicted in horror. The idea of snuff movies had terrified me ever since I first read urban legends about them online in the mid '90s. As an avowed cinephile, I'd long looked at filmgoing as something akin to a church service, where strangers congregated together to take part in something greater than themselves. Taken in that context, a snuff film would be the ultimate black mass—the greatest perversion of something meant to be pure and holy. What better subject for a horror movie? And, like Cronenberg before me, I too was a late-night TV junkie, abusing my parents' satellite and cable hookups to cruise the airwaves at all hours, anticipating what I might see next—and fearing what I might accidentally see. It was like David Cronenberg had cracked open my brain, looked inside, and cooked up Videodrome based on what he saw.

Over the years, I've returned again and again to *Videodrome*, finding both old comforts and something of new value each time; and, as I've become a horror writer myself, I've discovered it having influence on my own work, both explicit and subconscious. When I first began writing and submitting short horror stories to my college's literary magazine, all set against the backdrop of 1970s Times Square, one of my recurrent plot threads revolved around a forbidden snuff film said to be in the possession of an evil theater projectionist. Later, I'd write another story—never published, probably for the best—about the people responsible for the film, and it wasn't for nothing that the ceremonial outfits they wear to commit their cinematic crimes are described in a manner vaguely resembling the vestments worn by the Videodrome executioners. I've also tried to explore, for myself, some of the film's themes in my own work. Why are we drawn to horror? Does it speak to healthy or unhealthy desires? Why are sex and horror so inextricably linked not only in cinema, but also, apparently, the human mind? Without having seen Cronenberg explore these ideas first, I don't think I'd have thought more seriously about them myself—or had the courage to put my own spin on them.

(I'll interject here that, for all the other impact *Videodrome* has had on my life as an artist, it played no role in my working in optics for over seven years. Sometimes, things really are just coincidences).

That nostalgia factor has also had an impact on my work. Just as I've always found a sort of warped safety in the throwback world of *Videodrome*, I've always felt the most comfortably in my writing when it's been set in a version of the past I can endlessly manipulate and lose myself in—one of neons and new wave and all the lost promises of the Reagan era. It's no coincidence that my novel *Our Lady of the Inferno* is set in 1983, on the cusp of peak '80s-ness (that it was the same year *Videodrome* came out was a coincidence, and, though I struggled to find an organic way to drop a reference in, the movie had already disappeared from theaters and the pop culture consciousness by the time the book is set).

So, this has ultimately been a very long-winded way of saying that I'm the guy who finds comfort and inspiration in a sadomasochistic horror movie about snuff films and killer television; and I'm perfectly all right with that. It's a film I love endlessly, and which never ceases to leave me feeling fulfilled, intellectually or emotionally. And most importantly, I can say with much assurance that, without *Videodrome*, I would still be a writer, but definitely not the same one.

THE SHINING (1980)
BY
SADIE KATZ

Actress/Writer
Wrong Turn 6, Blood Feast (2016),
Bus Party to Hell, Scorned, Circus Road
Facebook/Instagram: @SadieKatz Twitter: @Sadie_Katz
SadieKatz.me

I'll be honest with you, I don't remember when I started enjoying horror films. However, I was a child of the '80s, therefore I was forced to watch them. I did enjoy the tamer scares of late night: *Tales from the Dark Side* (although the creepy opening always made me pee just a little), *Tales from the Crypt*, and *Monsters*, the show with the monster family eating popcorn around their TV to watch short tales of quirky terror. I mostly watched with my hands over my eyes and my fingers spread just enough to barely see out. I always ran thru my long hallway to get to my bedroom and couldn't look at our fireplace without thinking about a bloody Santa wielding an ax (thank you *Silent Night, Deadly Night*). At sleepovers with my neighbors (I'm talking about you Lisette and Lindsey), I begged them to rent a PG movie instead of horror (which of course, they never did).

I also always wanted to be an actress. The commitment level from the actors in horror was like nothing you'd see in other films. I'm not just talking about the screaming and begging, but the way the stories had a way of sticking with me for days. *A Nightmare on Elm Street* left me unable to sleep for weeks. But absolutely nothing prepared me for my favorite horror film ever...

THE SHINING

What's so strange and weird about *The Shining* is that it breaks the norm of most horror films, starting us off with Jack Torrance already being a pretty unlikable weirdo. Jack's son Danny is already weird as fuck, and we know his wife is essentially an abused woman. So, right at the onset, your stomach is in knots. Which is kinda the opposite of most horror films today - the normal setup is to look at a wonderfully happy family moving into this beautiful house and everything being great until the thirty minute mark, then...boom! Oh shit, it's haunted. Maybe at the film's opening, we get some scary death scene just to keep everyone's attention. But, this is Kubrick. He knows Jack Nicholson is already a strange bird, so he allows him to be just that. And this bird is about to be strangled.

In this film, Shelley Duvall is what a horror actress should really be on screen. Messy as fuck. I absolutely love her performance. The thing that drives me nuts about a lot of horror films now, and why I can watch them without covering my eyes, is that the girls are gorgeous and their makeup is perfect, with mascara smeared just enough to still be sexy; and yes, they're screaming and crying...blah blah blah. But, the camera and the audience are always aware of their beauty. By the way, I happen to find the beauty and genius in Shelley's casting to be her homeliness. Jack tends to eat scenes in what could be an almost comical way ("Here's Johnny!") Not that he's not totally fucking brilliant. But, if not for Shelley's absolute terror and her losing her mind - drooling, weeping, shaking for herself and her son - it would have changed the film. Her dread and fear is what the audience takes on and God, it's brilliant. Had Jack been chasing a buxom beauty with smeared mascara and a slight tremble, we would not have found him so absolutely fucking crazed in order to feel so damn sorry for her. I don't want to get into the stories of what Kubrick did to get that performance out of Duvall...that's for another book...but what's on-screen is brilliant.

A couple of months back, the lovely people of Cinespia did a screening of *The Shining*, so I took my 17-year-old son to see it. I figured, shit, I sleep with the lights off now, walk down my hallways with ease, and have written and starred in horror films. I can do this.

The lights on the packed theater go down, and we're off.

Jack at the office - those wicked eyebrows - the boy with the finger - REDRUM. My son is smiling. He's like, "This is unbelievable already." God, it really is. Had I ever noticed how incredible the sound design was before? How the blood spills around the elevator - those goddamned twins - the close up of Danny's wheels on the carpet - the bathtub scene - the lady going from young to old in Jack's arms - the ballroom - Jack typing - Jack following Shelley up the stairs with the ax - again the subliminal flashes of blood...suddenly I feel my hands covering my face, my fingers making space...just enough for my eyes.

I slept with the lights on...for weeks.

INSIDIOUS
BY
SCOTT DUNN

Actor/Writer/Director
Mandao Of The Dead, Schlep, Kickin' It
Twitter: @ScottyDunnIt Instagram: @ScottyDunnDidIt
MandaoFilms.com

I grew up in a religious household where horror movies weren't a regular thing for me. My wife saw *Child's Play* when she was six…so judge for yourself the differences in upbringing. I think the first horror movie I saw was *Psycho*. Great movie! It really taught me to love Alfred Hitchcock. Through him I learned about twists and suspense from movies like *The Birds, Rear Window,* and *Rope.* Jump forward to 1999 and everyone was talking about *The Sixth Sense.* One of my friends from youth group thought I should know that Bruce Willis was dead the whole time. Thanks Andrew…you're the reason I stopped going to youth group. Just kidding.

I liked that movie for so many reasons. One of them happened to be that the director, M. Night Shyamalan, was someone who made movies when he was just a young kid with a camcorder and a few friends. That's just like me! Look what a cool movie he crafted, I thought to myself.

I was going to do my essay on *The Sixth Sense*...and *Scream*...and *Psycho*...but when I gave it some more thought, I realized it had to be James Wan's *Insidious*. I needed to pick something that influenced me as a filmmaker today.

When I first saw *Insidious* in 2012 with my future wife Gina, I had no idea what to expect. It was a low-expectation watch. Those can be the most magical. I thought it was going to be a simple haunted house movie. James Wan is a talented director who has gone on to sharpen his skills over the years, but at the time, I still had *Saw* on my mind – a good movie, but not my favorite.

As *Insidious* rolled on, it took a turn into the realm of astral projection. Now I was getting hooked. I'd never seen a movie involving astral projection before. When I was growing up, my buddy used to tell me how awesome lucid dreaming was. It's where you realize you're dreaming and can control whatever you want within the dream. Astral projection is similar but the difference is that the astral realm is something that supposedly exists in real life. It's when you leave your body and travel around on this plane and the next. What a great tool for a horror movie...or any movie for that matter. The evil entity holding the youngest Lambert was fantastic. Known as the Lipstick-Face Demon, he looked like an evil Sith lord...but way scarier.

Also of note is how the movie didn't take itself too seriously. Yes it's a serious movie, but the ghost hunter characters of Tucker and Specs really gave it a comedic boost. The great Lin Shaye is SO good here. I really believed her as the intermediary between this reality and the next. I loved the astral realm created in *Insidious*. When the characters entered the realm, it took on a foggy and dreamlike property, like the deepest corner of your dreams. I really dug that the family banded together to get their son back from The Further. It was chilling and thrilling. Best of all, it was unique. It's a movie that makes me think about what is real and what is not.

Insidious contains what is imperative to a great horror movie – it can be watched over and over. It's not something that repulses you. It's something you want to invite in like a friend you're really comfortable with. It's like a cozy scary story you tell at a campfire or a sleepover. There's warmth to *Insidious*. Something about it makes you want to crawl up inside of it and hang out. I can't be the only one to feel that way. Also, its subject matter of astral projection is not just a made-up plot device. It's something that many people all over the world have claimed to experience. That makes it all the more tangible.

Fast-forward to 2018. I'm a writer/actor/director on the set of my second feature film entitled *Mandao of the Dead*. It's about a guy named Jay Mandao who uses astral projection to travel back in time to save his friends from imminent danger. It's a horror-comedy that was most definitely influenced by *Insidious*. I had written a different horror-comedy script that I was taking around LA and getting some mild interest from. I had some notable actors attached, along with some possible backing. When that backing fell through (along with a failed Kickstarter campaign), I was forced to go back to the drawing board. I kicked around ideas that I was passionate about. I decided I was going to have to self-fund the movie with what I had available: around $13,000 and some change. What could I do with that amount of money? I thought back to some of my favorite films in the horror genre. *Poltergeist* and *Insidious* instantly came to mind. Ironically enough, *Poltergeist* seems to have influenced *Insidious* quite a bit. It had a family with a supernatural problem that is haunting the youngest child. They have a medium, and her team, come in to try and rid the house of the problem.

I needed something to start with and astral projection jumped out at me. I wanted to explore that device while giving my movie a different angle than *Insidious*. Time travel. I would periodically refer back to *Insidious* for inspiration. James Wan and writer Leigh Whanell really nailed their approach on how they showed astral projection. Simplicity was their friend...and now it would be mine too. My movie has more of a sci-fi comedy vibe to it but the inspiration from *Insidious* is pivotal. As I said before, my budget was super low. I only had 2 sets to work with. Astral projection provided me a way to use those two sets and literally double and triple them. In my movie there's the real world, the astral realm, and different jumps in time. I don't know if I would've thought to utilize the sets that way if it hadn't been for the masterful approach James Wan and Leigh Whannell used for *Insidious*.

I'm honored that my movie is a part of the small list of films that involve astral projection. It's a fertile ground to explore. It doesn't hurt that *Insidious* was made for around 1.5 million dollars, which is a small budget for a Hollywood film for sure. James Wan has done big things with small budgets, which is really inspiring especially for someone like me who is steeped in the world of indie filmmaking. James Wan is not only Asian (I'm half Korean/Half Scottish), but he's someone who came up through the ranks by way of the independent film scene. He's a masterful director who thinks outside of the box and has definitely made his mark on the horror movie scene and beyond. He's a hero to me in many ways.

As a filmmaker, I'm reminded of how much *Insidious* influenced what I'm doing right now in my career. I'm making a trilogy of films exploring different ways my characters use astral projection. *Insidious* is, and continues to be, a beacon of how practical and minimal effects can be used. It inspired me to explore astral projection as a device for time travel. I have *Insidious* to thank for giving me an itch I've been very happy to scratch ever since. And for that, I will be eternally grateful.

EVIL DEAD II
BY
MICHAEL KALLIO

Writer/Director/Producer
Hatred of a Minute, Mutant Swinger from Mars,
Heart of Dorkness: The Making of My Name is Bruce,
Dinner with Leatherface
Facebook: @FilmMike
Instagram: @Michael.Kallio Twitter: @Darkallio

This story REALLY begins at, well...the beginning! As in, it STARTED with the original *Evil Dead*. As a kid, I didn't really LIKE horror films. Yeah, I said it. I'm writing an essay for a book ABOUT horror films and I don't like horror films? That was in the past...but I digress. Back then, I wasn't interested in the heart-pounding terror that I KNEW I would feel when watching something scary. I remember seeing *Raiders of the Lost Ark* and, while walking out of the theatre, my mother pointed out the one-sheet for *Poltergeist*. "Oooo! That looks scary! I want to see that!" she said. My response was a resounding "NOPE!" The few horror movies I could watch and tolerate were the more tragic and dramatic horror outings from Universal Studios such as *Frankenstein* or *The Wolfman* and the Edgar Allan Poe movies Roger Corman had produced. Those films had a gloomy and depressing tone. To me, the creatures and monsters were misunderstood and outcast from society, which I related to as a young artist and filmmaker. While some kids were playing baseball, I was writing and making movies with the neighbor kids. I was so obsessed with filmmaking, I would collect any and every newspaper article and movie ad I saw that had some relation to filmmaking in Michigan (even if it was about a horror film I thought I'd never see). It wasn't until I saw the first *Evil Dead* that I became desensitized almost immediately to anything horror.

I was attending a birthday party for a friend of mine named Mark. One of the activities of the night, aside from your usual cake and ice cream, was the viewing of a horror film. I figured I could do the cake and ice cream portion then blow out of there before the movie, but Mark had also invited Laura, a girl I was REALLY into at the time. "You're not going to let a horror movie scare you away from hanging out with Laura, are you?" was Mark's logic. It was sound logic. I reluctantly stayed. Who knows, maybe this would be a perfect opportunity to make out and I wouldn't have to WATCH the movie. Of course, that never happened, but what DID happen was something I never expected. I LOVED it. While Laura buried her head in my shoulders during all the perfect scary moments of the film, I laughed my ass off. I think I started to annoy the other people watching because I was having such a blast, I didn't even remember I was afraid of these kinds of movies (though DON'T get me started about *The Exorcist*...THAT is scary!). Needless to say, I was hooked, and thus began my journey into EVERYTHING horror! But I digress.

Between my now very frequent visits to the local video store (a great mom-and-pop place that had EVERYTHING from mainstream to totally obscure) renting anything and everything I read about in Fangoria magazine, I was going to every horror movie I could...*House, Night of the Creeps,* Cronenberg's *The Fly, Hellraiser, Aliens, The Lost Boys, Near Dark*...I couldn't stop. I HAD to see everything horror I could get my hands or eyeballs on. Some films I'd see two or three times in the same day. The one that eluded me was *Evil Dead II: Dead by Dawn.* I missed its initial limited theatrical release. I believe I was on a family vacation or something when it hit the one theatre in Michigan where it played for two weeks. Regardless of the story, I was upset that didn't get to see it. The sequel to the movie that numbed me of my fear of horror (minus *The Exorcist,* of course) had completely slipped by me. What the hell kind of horror fan was I that I could miss *Evil Dead II*? You, the reader, are probably wondering when the heck am I going to get to the point. Don't worry. We'll get there.

I scoured the pages of *Fango* for weeks, waiting for some announcement...ANY ANNOUNCEMENT about the release of the film that got away. After what felt like waiting an eternity for *Evil Dead II* to reach home video, it did. When I went to my local mom-and-pop video store to rent it, it wasn't there. No, not rented out. They DIDN'T have a copy. The copy they ordered didn't come with their recent shipment. Searching other more mainstream video stores in my area didn't help. It was like this movie didn't want me to see it. I was bummed to say the least. The end...just kidding.

So, after another what-seemed-like-forever (okay, it was a week. Hey, I was a teenager - everything's more dramatic), I finally rented *Evil Dead II: Dead by Dawn.* I could call it a "game changer," or I could say it "was the most impactful horror movie I'd ever seen," but no, this was different. It was beyond a horror film. It changed the way I thought of camera movements and how the camera, especially in a film such as this, can BE a character. Kudos to Bruce Campbell, our reluctant semi-action hero who gave a performance that was both incredibly dramatic and downright hilarious as both the Deadites and his friend and director, Raimi, brutalized him. I had seen horror comedy films before, but nothing like this. I consumed every weird nuance and bizarre nook and cranny. This was a "horror" film on another level. Things like the Farewell to Arms book on top of the trash can that Ash uses to cover his possessed severed hand, or the "Eyeball/Flyball" moment when Bobby Jo chokes on a flying eyeball - THESE were moments of inspired brilliance. The entire concept of Ash being somewhat of an inept, accidental anti-hero, going beyond what was explored in the first movie, was a touch of genius. When Ash emerges from the cellar to confront the possessed Henrietta (played exquisitely by Ted Raimi), with his heroic, perfectly-placed bleeding cut that gave him his gallant uni-brow and whistles at the demon egging her on for a fight, I cheered! I adored this movie so much, I had it playing in the background during my high school graduation party. I watch this movie at least once a month and at least twice around Halloween. I still love Bruce Campbell's performance and I worship Sam Raimi's direction to this day. This was high-octane, punk rock, horror filmmaking at its best (well, aside from the actual "punkrockness" of *Return of the Living Dead*). It was also the moment I said to myself, "I will work with these guys..." - these guys being Bruce Campbell, Rob Tapert and Sam Raimi. Who knew I would actually become part of an extended film family? I sure as heck didn't. It all began with a letter...sort of.

Around 1989-90, some things happened that started the weird "snowball" effect based on some sort of serendipity that became my very real connection to the whole *Evil Dead/Evil Dead II* world. I worked on my first made-in-Michigan horror movie *Hellmaster* as a production assistant, which introduced me to some amazing special FX makeup people, Jeff and Roger, who I ended up working with for many years. My buddy Jeff introduced me to Gary Jones, one of the many talented effects people that worked on *Evil Dead II*. I won BEST COSTUME at the first Fangoria Convention in Dearborn, Michigan where Bruce Campbell was the celebrity judge with a *Darkman* getup I made. I believe it was the same year I told Tony Timpone, editor of *Fangoria Magazine*, that I was going to be in the pages of

Fango someday (right, Tony?).

One night while watching *Evil Dead II*, I got a call from my high school pal Erin. He talked me into going on a blind date, which wasn't something I was in the mood for after a recent breakup. Reluctantly, I went. It was one of them fancy blind dates...you know, the kind you get sort of dressed up for. We picked up my "date" and went to some artsy picture at the Detroit Film Theatre located within the Detroit Institute of Arts. Fancy schmancy to say the least! Our night ended at The Whitney, an old haunted historical mansion in downtown Detroit, which had been converted into a high-end restaurant. We made reservations for the top floor, where they served extravagant desserts and coffees so we could hang out, discuss the movie and make small talk. What movie we saw, I can't remember, but the desserts were tasty and the coffee quite good. It didn't take long for my date (whose name I can't remember either) and I to realize we weren't the slightest bit compatible. I talked about my love of film - especially *Evil Dead II* - Sam Raimi's style and Bruce Campbell's crazy performance. My date, however, didn't understand my dreams of Hollywood and proceeded to tell me in an almost jealous way that Hollywood was 3000 miles away from Detroit and I probably didn't have a shot. That's not something I, let alone anyone, wants to hear. I excused myself for a moment and went to the men's room to take a breather...I needed to clear my head of the negative. Any artistic type knows EXACTLY what I'm talking about.

As I walked to the second floor where the closest restrooms were located, there was a small crowd gathered near the bar. They were listening to two performers, a gentleman tickled the ivories on a beautiful grand piano accompanied by a woman singing a cabaret style version of *The Little Mermaid* classic "Under the Sea." I stopped for a moment. The woman looked SO familiar to me. Apparently, I was there for longer than a moment because when I turned around, my date was standing there with a strange jealous girlfriend look on her face. I guess I was busted, because when I returned from the restroom, both girls had gone downstairs to wait by the valet. "I guess there won't be a second date," I said. Erin laughed and proceeded to tell me my date had become offended because she caught me eyeing the older woman singing on the second floor. As we headed downstairs, I saw the singer one more time and it hit me. THAT'S ELLEN SANDWEISS FROM *EVIL DEAD*! I pointed out to Erin that she was the actress violated by the woods in the original *Evil Dead* movie, which was why I was staring like a stalker.

The ride back to my date's house was awkward to say the least. We sat mainly in silence. Every once in a while, Erin would try and cut through the tension with little results. As she exited the car, I shook her hand, which she seemed hesitant to do. With as much rudeness she could muster, my date's last words to me were an incredibly sarcastic, "Good luck." At first, it didn't bother me and I laughed it off, but after a few weeks, I couldn't get her bitchy words out of my head. It was if she challenged me to take initiative and prove her wrong. So I took a chance and wrote Bruce Campbell a letter asking for advice about raising money for a feature film. *Evil Dead* made me seek out horror but *Evil Dead II* made me dig for information (which I had been subconsciously doing for years). I wanted the how-to knowledge of raising money like the Renaissance Pictures guys did. How did a bunch of schmoes from Michigan go from Super-8 filmmaking - like I used to do - to the superb horror comedy *Evil Dead II* and beyond?

Three weeks later, as I was rushing to a meeting to get seed money for my first feature film project, the phone rang. It was he...Bruce Campbell. I was so shocked, I dropped the phone. Here I am, talking to the star of my favorite horror movie and he agrees to pass on his knowledge and become not just a "mentor" but also my "tor-mentor." Four and a half years later, I began production on my first feature film, *Hatred of a Minute*, with one of my idols and now friend Bruce Campbell as my producer (and maybe a few cameos buried within), also starring another pal I made along the way, Gunnar Hansen, famous for playing Leatherface in *The Texas Chain Saw Massacre*. *Evil Dead II* was a constant source of inspiration during filming. I wanted to be as creative in my direction as I could and strived to make my crazy little psychological thriller/horror film have some of the kinetic energy *Dead by Dawn* possessed throughout the film. Although *Hatred* and *Evil Dead II* are very different, I aspired to that less conventional way of shooting, which gave a little more momentum to my first flick.

So there's the story (or many small anecdotes) of my love and strange connection to *Evil Dead II* (and *Evil Dead*, etc.). I'm humbled and blessed to be in this world and have connection to my favorite horror movie on this level and it continues to this day. I guess that sarcastic "good luck" my blind date threw at me was really luck after all. I work with Bruce regularly. He's practically family to me now. I worked with the Ladies of The *Evil Dead* on a documentary about their return to acting. I shot archival footage for the 20th anniversary screening of *Evil Dead*. I directed the behind-the-scenes documentary for *My Name is Bruce* in which I also have a small role. I even somehow ended up with one of the magnifying glass necklaces and a matte painting from *Evil Dead II*. The movie truly is a masterpiece. It's like Tex Avery and The Three Stooges dropped acid and made a horror movie together. Though I am a horror lover and have quite a few films that I could consider my "favorite," I always go to *Evil Dead II* as my true go-to favorite and, much like *Jaws*, it's one of those movies I have to watch any time and at any point it's on. *Evil Dead II: Dead by Dawn* is GROOVY! Yeah. I had to go there.

ADAM CHAPLIN

BY

JOEL HODGE

Cinematographer
Bellflower, Canary, Snake Outta Compton,
Movies and Machines, Chuck Hank and the San Diego Twins
Instagram: @JoelHodge Coatwolf.com

A s a young lad, I remember finally talking my mom into letting me see *Child's Play 2* in the theater. When we got there, I took one look at the poster and was terrified. I begged her to take me home instead. This was back when movies were still scary; back when you weren't sure if they were real or not. Watching movies as a kid was a whole different ball game.

I remember the first time I watched *Predator*. My uncle popped the VHS in the VCR while my mom was at work. It was the best day of my life. Still might be.

Remember when there were all these movies you weren't allowed to see?

The biggest, "I'm not supposed to be watching this" moment though, was when I saw the first *Evil Dead*. I was a freshman in high school and had made friends with a senior who had a copy of it on VHS. Though not an official copy, it was recorded onto a blank VHS tape over the top of Saturday morning cartoons. This was a big deal. He couldn't talk about how he got it, but one night when I stayed over at his place, we watched it. That shit blew my mind. The gore? The violence? I had never seen anything like it. That movie sent me down a path that has guided my life ever since. A few years later, I got my hands on *Evil Dead 2*--which is still one of my all-time favorites--then I found *Dead Alive*, and the list goes on from there. The point is, back then, when you got your hands on one of these gems, they were naughty. You had this feeling like you weren't supposed to be seeing it.

Now, 20 years later, that feeling is long since gone. Those images from *Evil Dead* and *Dead Alive* (or *Braindead* if you're from across the pond) have stayed with me my entire life: Ash battling his hand; using his teeth to tear off a strip of duct tape; Lionel slaughtering a house full of zombies with a lawn mower; and then there's the infamous custard scene...Those moments will always stick with me. Since then, life has been lame, weak, and gore-free.

Then I found *Adam Chaplin*.

I saw it about five years ago and its imagery still rings in my head. It's the first movie I recommend when anyone is looking for bizarre gore, violence, and insanity. Everything about this film screamed out to me as if all the old low budget gore-fests from my past had a mutated stepchild that was meaner, uglier, and more violent than all of them.

The story is simple: revenge. But it's how he gets it done that is so brutal. The visual style is so creepy, low budget, and stylized. I instantly thought, "what the fuck is this?" It didn't take long before I was literally looking over my shoulder as if my mom was going to be there to make me turn it off. It felt taboo, like something I shouldn't be watching. Like a good horror film should feel.

If you enjoy mutilation, violence, gore, fist fights, gun violence, monsters, skull crushing, buff dudes, more violence and more gore, this is the movie for you. It is a live-action love letter to the anime *Fist of the North Star*. To be honest, it's really hard to watch at times. There are some flashbacks that look like I shot them when I was in high school. But the hard work, time, and dedication it must have taken to pull off all the insanity in this film, is truly amazing. The team that put this together are fucking heroes for caring so much about the violence. I can't imagine what they went through and I'm proud of them. God bless them, and God bless *Adam Chaplin*.

DERANGED
BY
SHANE BITTERLING
Writer
Beneath Loch Ness, Reel Evil (aka Specters),
Desperate Escape, Weedjies, Hell Comes to Hollywood
Twitter/Facebook: @ShaneBitterling
Instagram: @Shane_Bitterling

It's always been in vogue to blame one's mother for all of the strife in their life. In my case, my mother is to blame for everything that I hold dear, for better or worse, I still don't know. Mom, Laura Bitterling, was never a true horror fanatic, but had just enough of a sinister cinema streak to creep out the men closest to her. On an early teenage date, she insisted they go see the new Alfred Hitchcock movie, *Psycho*, at The Isis, their local theater in Winamac, Indiana. My dad obliged, as Bitterling boys have always known that taking a young lady to a horror movie is sure-fire bet for some hand holding and potential arm squeezing. Neither were ready for *Psycho*. Dad walked Mom home, traipsing several miles through the dark-

ness, woods, hooting owls overhead, and looming Norman
Bateses behind every tree, all the way to her house. This was
the last horror movie he wanted to see, with the exception of
Grizzly (1976), my first ever theatrical experience – thank you,
folks! "Bears don't count. That's nature," he said. Hitchock
twisted my mom into such a wad that our family was never allowed to take showers - only baths. Her reasoning was that the
shower nozzle didn't work. Well into college, my brother tried
it for the first time. It worked like a dandy. It was only then that
she came clean about her fear of being spectacularly stabbed to
death while standing under the showerhead. Apparently, that
could never happen while sitting like a lump in the tub.

Born at the very tail end of the Monster Kid Kraze, my
brother and I had bedrooms filled with Aurora monster model
kits, Mego monster figures, and posters of Frankenstein, purchased from Captain Company in the pages of *Famous Monsters of Filmland*. We loved our monsters. I can't pinpoint the
exact moment I became a horror lover, though it wasn't thrust
on me. I suppose I leeched it from the environment organi-
cally, which I still feel is the best, true way to get that type of
jolly. Although I was surrounded by them, I found them scary
as all hell. Mom would stay up late on the weekend to watch
Nightmare Theatre, Indiana's local horror package show, with
the unmatchable Sammy Terry as the host. Sammy didn't play
it for gags and corny bits. He was unique amongst the horror
hosts. He was truly, deeply scary. I'd watch as much as I could
through my fingers or from under a blanket, but usually tapped
out halfway through (my quickest exit being five minutes into
George A. Romero's *Night of the Living Dead*). Bill Hinzman's
graveyard zombie was too much for me, and to be honest, I
can't watch that movie without reverting back to that little kid
and getting scared at that scene. I was scared as hell, but it was
a thrill I haven't shaken to this day.

My mom, the superwoman that she is, watched the entire
thing. "They were eating each other!" she said, about how awful it was and how it really got to her. "But it wasn't like that

Psycho. Yeesh."

By the early '80s, I was full into my horror obsession. Give me what you got. I can take it. I combed through the TV Guide, circling all the late night horror fare that I needed to see. But the movie that scared my parents so bad never invaded the listings.

Then it happened. One of the channels had a Hitchcock marathon lasting several weeks. I finally saw *Psycho.* Mom watched it with me. Dad had no interest. While I thought it was as perfect a movie as could be, I was already watching things with a higher body count and full viscera on display. I didn't think it was that scary. I mean, not Bill Hinzman scary. Not shower banning scary, anyway.

Then, she told me this tale of my uncle. And those tales usually end up bad, legendary or both. He had moved to Beloit, Wisconsin in the early '70s. Mom and dad drove up to see him for the weekend. Every few miles on a station break between songs, they heard a radio ad for a movie so heinous, she kept repeating, "I'll never see THAT movie. No way, sir."

As they got to my uncle's place, he told them he wanted to go to the drive-in theater not far away. With the drive-in always being one of our family's favorite outings, they went along. It turns out, the movie showing was the one that she heard the ad for all those hundreds of miles. That movie was called *Deranged: Confessions of a Necrophile.*

She went on to tell me how evil that movie was. So scarring, she buried it deep into her brain and wouldn't let it out, no matter how much it knocked about those years. "He dug up his mother and killed these cute gals for their skin and stuff. And he wore their skin, too. And made drums out of it. And there's a scene where he's feeding her and she pukes up all this green junk and…it's just awful. Goddamn your uncle for making us go to that." She had the physical willies as she spoke about it. Now you're talking my language, mama.

Deranged became my new obsession. A movie so rotten to the core that it broke the strongest woman I know. I hunted every video store in a wide area, only to come back empty-handed. I asked if it could be purchased. It couldn't. Not only could I not find the movie, I couldn't find anything about it. No images in the monster books, *Fangoria* or otherwise.

At the time, I was dabbling in special effects make-up in the garage, inspired by movies and a copy of Dick Smith's *Do-It-Yourself Monster Make-up Handbook* I scored through a magazine. I wasn't good, and materials were impossible to come by, but I was determined to make this my future. And then I was able to nab a copy of *Grande Illusions*, the how-to make-up book by my monster hero, Tom Savini. Holy crap! An entire chapter on *Deranged*, which was the first movie Savini worked on. There it was. Proof positive that this thing existed.

I knew what those effects looked like and learned all of Savini's techniques on how he built the corpses and such, but I was still unable to see them in play.

My obsession was growing deeper. And if being a horror fan breeds anything at all, it's obsession. The need to see everything. Hear everything. Physically own everything.

For a birthday in the late '80s, I saw a VHS sized, wrapped gift. I hoped upon hope it was a copy of this grail. With one eye squinted, I peeled the wrapping back and saw the first few letters that would spell *Deranged*. But it ended up being the one directed by Chuck Vincent in 1987. A $79.99 swing and a miss.

All hope was lost until 1993, when my new issue of *Film Threat* magazine came in the mail. I flipped through it to see what articles I would read first and came across a black and white ad from Moore Video, which was offering up a first-time released, completely uncut copy of *Deranged* with a bonus documentary. Bonus features didn't exist then, except Charles Band's *Videozone*, which was a better film school than the one I was attending.

I immediately sent in a money order, eyeballed that mailbox from the window for weeks, and then it came. I called mom and told her that I had finally found it. "Don't bring it around here," she reacted.

Nobody else in my college house shared in the excitement,

and I didn't care for the oncoming comments during the movie, so I popped the tape into the VCR and, within seconds, I was completely taken aback. What was this?

I'd gained enough knowledge of the movie at that point to somewhat know what I was getting into. Savini was a hero. Bob Clark was already a favorite filmmaker, with *Porky's, A Christmas Story, Murder by Decree* and even *Turk 182*. I was then unable to see *Black Christmas*, which is a perennial. He deemed this project too gruesome for him to direct, so played an uncredited producer role here. The director, Alan Ormsby, here with co-director Jeff Gillen (frequent collaborator and Santa from *A Christmas Story*), and Clark collaborated on a previous favorite, *Children Shouldn't Play with Dead Things*.

My expectations were high for horrendous horror. But this...this is a comedy. Something my mom had forgotten. Or maybe something she never realized.

One thing I'm certain of is that she didn't make the connection between *Psycho* and *Deranged*. Both were inspired by the real life serial killer, Ed Gein, The Butcher and Ghoul of Plainfield, whose atrocities ended in 1957 with his arrest. You know the tales. He was the Midwest boogeyman for decades. Even though he was institutionalized until his death in 1986, he could be anywhere. He was always waiting in the woods. He was sitting next to you at the diner. He was the guy next door. Everybody looked like Ed Gein in the Midwest. And everybody was him. He and Charles Manson were giggling in the barn, sharpening their tools, and making pajamas from the skin of some hapless victim.

So what in the hell is this comedy I'm watching? The movie begins with a serious but somewhat corny reporter, who fills us in on some of the backstory. It's that "you are there" style that I have come to love, akin to Charles B. Pierce's *Legend of Boggy Creek* and *The Town that Dreaded Sundown*. They fit somewhere between documentary and a linear form of storytelling.

The opening scenes of Ed Gein (known here as Ezra Cobb, the greatest name in all of horror) and his mother are sick, twisted, and funny. Yes, mom, she does barf up that green stuff aplenty and it is gross, but played for Grand Guignol laughs. His interactions with the locals are also played for hoots.

Despite my initial shock, I was immediately roped in. Those people were so realistic. I knew each and every one. The locations were homes, diners and shops that I frequented in the Heartland. No wonder this scared my mom so much, especially given that she saw it at the drive-in not far from where Gein lived. Despite the often boisterous humor, it was burrowing into my marrow as well. It was all very familiar; one of the first movies that felt like it was happening just outside my window. It was down the street. It was next door.

There is a sadness and oppressive feeling of isolation rolling through the entirety of *Deranged* from the start: the stark winter snow blanketing everything; the lone houses without a neighbor for miles; a local shop that doesn't appear to be connected to a town; the quietness of it all; the Carl Zittrer score, (which is comprised of Bible hymns played on an organ, sounds less like a soundtrack than a far away Sunday mass wafting with the chill); the constant wind through the windows. It makes you feel alone. Just silence, loneliness and a feeling of crushing cold. You understand why Ezra was driven to do the things he did. Well, kinda. You can't replicate those things in movies today. Equipment is too high-tech. There's no life to the sound. The visuals are too crisp (or degraded too much) and the cinematography too aware. It's all too clean, clinical and lifeless. It all created an atmosphere that was a little bit by design, and a lot by just being made in that time on a low budget.

And then there's Ezra, roaming through that world, played with awkward perfection by Roberts Blossom (Christine, Home Alone), with his sunken features, weathered skin, wide eyes and good ol' boy demeanor. It is one of my favorite roles by any actor, horror or otherwise. And a role Blossom would never talk about during his career. He's a mother-beaten, miserably lonely man who isn't comfortable in his own skin, only finding happiness in wearing the flesh of others. It's only then when he seems alive and confident. A standout scene is when he shows his handiwork to Sally (in the form of a drum made from a belly and the drumstick being a femur), whom he has decided will take the place of his dearly departed mother. It's a very frightening scene, taking a wholly different, but equally unnerving approach to a similar scene from the other 1974 Gein inspired classic, *The Texas Chain Saw Massacre*.

Whereas Psycho, *The Texas Chain Saw Massacre* and *The Silence of the Lambs* used Gein as a jumping off point for inspiration, *Deranged* is the closest depiction of the Gein story to this day. Using a journalistic approach to display the madness, winding the viewer tight as we get to that excruciating ending, which doesn't end on a visual, but a bit of audio, courtesy of Ezra, that is bona fide bone jangling.

It was sometime during this movie, with its stripped down cinema, that it dawned on me that monsters aren't scary. People are scary. I see four or five Ezra's on my way to class. My town is filled with them. Anyone of them could be a killer. There's no use looking under the bed for monsters. The killer comes knocking on your door, wearing a straw hat.

There have been several home video editions of *Deranged* since that Moore VHS – which was stolen with a bunch of other tapes in school – and I'm always eager to show it to other horror fans and fiends, but rarely get any takers. I don't believe I've been able to introduce it to anybody in almost twenty years, believe it or not. Despite all the spiff and shined up boxes, the movie still remains a bit of an obscurity. Perhaps this is why I love it so much. Horror fanatics are obsessive, weird creatures. We want to share our experiences with others in the freakshow, but also want that coveted prize all our own so nobody can tarnish it by having the masses adopt it. I can't quite place my finger on it, but I can point to everything that I love within it. It's a family thing. It's mine because nobody else wants it. I root for the underdog. And like poor ol' Ezra, I can thank my mama for making me this way. She didn't know it, but she put Gein in the veins.

THE BIRDS

BY
CHARLES WINECOFF

Author
Split Image: The Life of Anthony Perkins

E ven though I was born in New York City the year *Psycho* was released, I still got to experience the best of 1950s Americana thanks to the (then) still new invention known as television (with rabbit ears). Atomic monster movies like *Them!*, *The Giant Claw*, *Tarantula*, and *The Deadly Mantis* played on an endless loop as constant reminders of the dangerous games Cold War mankind played with mother nature.

For a nerdy kid like me, who was a walking encyclopedia of horror trivia, it was heaven. Sleepovers at my best friend's house were our own Manhattan version of camping, lying on blankets in the living room as we struggled to stay up until 3 AM to catch *The Giant Gila Monster* on the Late Late Late Late Show.

These creepy crawler movies all followed the same formula: a scientific mishap (often a faulty nuclear blast) unleashes an over-sized pest, causing a handsome scientist and his lovely assistant (or vice versa) to investigate, fall in love, and narrowly avoid death-by-bug until the US military finally incinerates the creature. There was comfort in the guarantee of a problem solved - life back to normal and no hair out of place for Mara Corday.

So naturally, when Hitchcock's *The Birds* made its network TV debut in 1968, I was stoked. My dad put aside his usual fare - *Star Trek* or *Batman* or *The Wild, Wild West* - to watch it with me. I had never seen a Hitchcock movie before, and this one sounded like my cup of tea. Boy, was I in for a surprise.

Even then, *The Birds* wasn't really scary (except for the eyes-pecked-out-at-the-farmhouse scene, the film's one gory jolt). The violence was exciting, sure, but in between the famous set pieces (bird bombardments on the children's party, the school, the telephone booth, etc.) the film's nonchalant, slow-burn sense of doom was deeply unsettling - especially for a spoiled American child raised on a diet of postwar Hollywood bromides.

Hitchcock revised the Atomic Age sci-fi rules in three big ways: 1) he made the "invaders" prosaic, everyday, even cute critters; 2) he offered no explanation as to why our feathered friends turned homicidal; and 3) he demonstrated that absolutely no one is safe - not even a charming, perfectly-coiffed movie star like Tippi Hedren. In Hitchcock's world, unlike that of Jack Arnold, beauty is no shield against brutality, pain, or nature gone berserk.

I had not yet seen *Psycho*, in which he butchered Marion Crane, his heroine, in the first 30 minutes. But in *The Birds*, what he does to socialite Melanie Daniels is almost worse: he rips away all of her egotistical defenses - her wit and sex appeal - reducing her to a bloody, scarred, catatonic mess. She is left mentally and physically broken, with no promise that she will recover or make it to safety. That never happened in a giant spider movie.

Hitchcock's violation of the unspoken lookers-don't-die

code freaked me out far more than any bird blitzkrieg.

Tattered, Melanie and the Brenners cautiously drive off in her tiny, canvas-topped Aston Martin into an ominous landscape of clucking fowl. Their future doesn't look bright. Fade to black. No happy ending.

I urgently asked my dad, "Why are the birds attacking? Where is the family going? Are they going to be alright?" Not even my father had any answers. I'd never experienced that kind of uncertainty. It wasn't in our American lexicon. That ambiguous non-ending frightened me in a profound way.

Death, at least, is final. But an iffy destiny of just more suffering? Hey, that's life, kiddo. Get used to it.

But you don't need to be eight years old to be perplexed by *The Birds*. What is this purported "horror movie" really all about? It begins as a brisk romantic comedy, then descends inexorably into darkness. (Does this say something about romantic love?) As for plot - what plot? As Hedren sighs to her new friend (and rival) in Bodega Bay, played by Suzanne Pleshette, "Oh, it all seems so pointless."

Hitchcock scatters clues throughout as to what the point might be. During the climactic attic attack, for instance, in which Melanie vainly fights off a room full of angry crows and gulls, there is almost no dialogue. But as bloody Melanie loses her battle, becoming more and more delirious before collapsing under the onslaught, she utters a few broken, incoherent phrases - "Is Cathy in the...get out of here!" - that reveal what she's thinking of in her last moments of consciousness: not of saving herself, but of getting Mitch's 11-year-old sister Cathy (Veronica Cartwright) to safety. Stripped of all her smug trappings, wealthy, wounded Melanie's basic goodness finally shines through.

That seems to be the moral of *The Birds*: that behind our hurt and our emotional armor, human beings care for and need each other. But the Master of Suspense doesn't clobber us with the message the way Stanley Kramer or Spielberg would. No cheap sentiment for him. He dispassionately leaves it up to us to figure it out for ourselves.

Unlike every other Hollywood movie, *The Birds* has no musical score to signal how we are supposed to feel about any of the characters, their relationships, or even about the attacks. Like a great painting - and Robert Burks' muted color cinematography certainly qualifies as art - *The Birds* stands matter-of-factly on its own terms, open to interpretation (or not).

Think about that. Here you have an A-list, million dollar movie held to absolutely none of the conventions of the studio system or the genre. No plot. No explanation. No score. No mushy romance (Hedren and Rod Taylor have little chemistry). No tidy wrap up. No end titles either. What did Hitchcock think he was doing?

If *Psycho* was his campaign to conquer European neorealism (Clouzot's *Les Diaboliques*), *The Birds* is his foray into the avant-garde. It's almost a sister film to Antonioni's *L'Avventura*, a similarly nebulous (yet compelling) meditation on the meaning of life (or lack thereof). There's even a dash of Fellini when Melanie Daniels, having just arrived in Bodega Bay, sets out in her rented dinghy wearing high heels, a mink coat, and carrying a bird cage. The only thing missing is Nino Rota.

How Hitchcock managed to convince the suits at Universal to finance this surreal art project - with a total unknown in the starring role - is one of the feats of Hollywood history.

Six decades haven't made *The Birds'* virtuosic special effects laughable or its enigmatic poetry any less relevant. But just imagine how reverentially it would be regarded if it had been pulled from release for a few years the way Hitchcock's flawed masterpiece *Vertigo* was (and let's be honest: that Disney-esque animated nightmare sequence has not aged well).

Risen from the lowlife kitsch of the Atomic Age, *The Birds* endured decades of promiscuous local affiliate broadcasts with crude commercial breaks and survived the advent of CGI without losing any of its menacing, poignant edge. That's what happens when you break those pesky things that are meant to be broken in the first place.

Still, don't take your eight-year-old to see it. It's really for adults only.

MISERY
BY
LARA JEAN

Actor, Dancer, Singer, Producer
60 Seconds to Die, 2 Jennifer,
Ugly Sweater Party, Bong Appetit, Sesame Street Live
Instagram/Facebook: @LaraJeanOfficial

I remember the setting perfectly. I was sitting on the old brown carpet of my parents' family room with my back against their brown leather couch. The lights were dim. The room was cold. I was wrapped in an old blanket my Nana had knitted for me when I was a child. The trees outside my living room window scratched on the glass as the beginning credits rolled on my dad's 1980s TV screen. I had no idea what I was getting myself into, but by the end, I was hooked. When I first saw *Misery*, I had never read the book it was adapted from. My mom had read all of Stephen King's books at the time, and she would tell me about his stories and how detailed his characters were. She knew how much I loved horror and urged me to watch Misery. So when it was set to play on the television one night, I made sure to be free. What really intrigued me right from the start was the fact that the film did not credit any of the actors during the first 2 minutes. This was the first film I saw that did that. It also used no music. There was nothing on the screen but the scene right from the start. I was pulled right into the world of novelist Paul Sheldon, played by James Caan. It wasn't until he finished his untitled book and reached for his celebratory cigarette that the music finally started, and it fit perfectly (score by Marc Shaiman). Paul Sheldon soon suffers a serious car crash and is rescued by Annie Wilkes (Kathy Bates). Annie brings him to her cabin to recover and claims to be his biggest fan, but the film takes a dark turn when she discovers Sheldon is killing off her favorite character. It is said Annie suffers from extreme Bipolar Disorder, and that, mixed with possibly being a celebrity stalker, stirs up some problems.

She quickly became my favorite character in horror. As an actor, I dream of one day having a role like that. Bates has the ability to bring into the scene, making you feel like she's standing right there with you. This was the first time I ever saw a woman as a lead in horror...and as the killer! This film inspired me to pursue my dreams as an actor and, to this day, pushes me to not give up as a performer. I always struggled with the way I looked. I always felt I was never good enough, but Kathy Bates as Annie Wilkes made me the happiest girl alive the day I saw her on that screen in *Misery*. The fact that the girl next door could be your neighborhood stalker? The idea that horror could come from anywhere? At first, this was very shocking to me, but also very eye-opening. *Misery* opened my mind to new characters that could be and, one day, will be. Thank you Kathy Bates! Thank you for your amazing performance. I am inspired by you every morning that I step into rehearsal. I am inspired by you every time I step in front of an audience. I am inspired by *Misery*, and will continue to be for the rest of my life.

To all my beautiful performers out there, don't let the negative get you down. There is a role for everyone. If you can't find it, make it!! Remember, *Misery* doesn't have to mean what you think. For me, it was a change of a lifetime.

M- Magical
I- Inspiring
S- Serenity
E- Emerging
R- Relief
Y- Yearning

Now I sit here, not on my parents carpet, but on my own, leaning against a big white bed, looking down at a new script that has been handed to me, using *Misery* as my character inspiration. One day, I hope there will be a girl that sees me like I saw Kathy Bates in *Misery*. I hope I inspire in her what Bates inspired in me. Shout out to my mom and all women everywhere! We got this!

BLOOD FEAST (1963)

BY
JOE CASTRO

Director/Producer/Special Effects Artist
Blood Feast 2: All U Can Eat, Terror Toons, Xenophobia,
The Summer of Massacre, The Jackhammer Massacre
Facebook: @Joe.Castro Instagram: @ Joe_Castro_Director

Over 5 decades ago, the industry of making slasher and splatter movies was very different than it is today...actually, it was nonexistent. We still must remember and pay homage to Herschell Gordon Lewis' *Blood Feast*, the original 1963 splatter/slasher movie. Why is this - without a doubt - the original slasher film? Because *Blood Feast* is the first movie to exploit blood in color, and the first to use the story of a deranged killer/psychopath who stalks innocent victims, one by one, killing each one in a gruesome, horrible, on-screen death, only to die at the hands of the hero or heroine of the film in the climax by an even more horrific death!

Does that storyline sound familiar? Of course it does. It has been duplicated, copied, Xeroxed, and imitated in every subsequent slasher/splatter movie since this original film. (E.g.: *Friday the 13th, A Nightmare on Elm Street, The Texas Chain Saw Massacre, Hellraiser, Halloween,* etc.)

Herschell Gordon Lewis, better known as "The Godfather of Gore," has done so much for the genre. It would be a crime to not include him in every horror movie list compilation and homage. The film was written, produced, and directed by Herschel, he also created all of the special effects gore, as well as scoring the entire movie with original music. Herschell is, was, and forever shall be a true master of his craft.

Here is a WARNING to all first time viewers: some of the special effects in the film were created using real animal organs and body parts. I, myself, am a special effects artist of 37 years. Today, in the year 2019, we would never use real animal parts for special effects on a movie screen for our entertainment. Today, we have the technology to reproduce these things in a special effects studio that look absolutely real, without using real animal parts. I consider it very taboo to waste the body of an animal for our entertainment. Times have changed and, while I respect what Herschell has done for our genre, I encourage all independent filmmakers who make slasher/splatter movies to never use real animal parts in their films. We must learn from our past.

In 2001, I had the honor of creating all of the special effects for the sequel to *Blood Feast, Blood Feast 2: All You Can Eat,* also directed by Herschell Gordon Lewis. In secrecy, Herschell revealed to me the blood formula he used in the original 1963 film. I hold it very dear to my heart, and still use it when creating gore and blood effects for other directors' films as a respectful homage to Herschell and all that he has done for us.

Blood Feast is a definite must-see for all independent filmmakers in the horror movie genre. If you have not seen this film, your education into the world of slasher and horror movies is definitely incomplete!

NIGHT OF THE LIVING DEAD
(1968)
BY
STEVE "UNCLE CREEPY" BARTON

Producer, Writer, Actor, Journalist, Radio Host
*Never Sleep Again: The Elm Street Legacy, The Amityville Murders, George A. Romero's Survival of the Dead,
Brainwaves Horror and Paranormal, Dread Central*
Facebook/Twitter: @UncleCreepy
Instagram: @UncleCreepyBW

*N*ight of the Living Dead. There are so many very different reasons why this is - and always will be - my favorite movie of all time, bar none!

To explain why that is, we're gonna need to go way, waaayyyyy back. I was born at 1:34 AM. Given that the first time I ever took my first breath was in the middle of the night, you could probably guess that yes, I am a night owl. Always have been, always will be. I'll never forget one particular moment in time. Some people have their defining moment late in their lives. Usually sometime during adulthood. Me? I'm fucking weird, man. I had mine at age three. That's right, three!

Even at a young age, I knew that the night was a special time. When the sun went down, all bets were off. Reality took a backseat to the darkness. Anything could be lurking there... creeping through the world at all ungodly hours. I dug the possibilities. I was never scared of the dark but was always curious as to what it may be hiding. As children, my brother Rob and I used to have a simple M.O.: when we would hear our parents snoring, it was our cue to run to the living room and pop on the TV. The coolest shit ever would play in the middle of the night. I loved old '50s and '60s horror and sci-fi. Monsters were magical to me, like unicorns. If I had to pick a second favorite horror flick, it would no doubt be the original *Frankenstein*. I always related to Frankenstein's Monster. He never asked to be here; yet, here he was...forsaken by his father, just like I was. How could I NOT understand him? Late night TV was like forbidden fruit to Rob and I, and we'd watch it as much and as quietly as possible.

One night though...I was alone. My parents were snoring up a storm. I got out of bed and tiptoed to the living room, ninja-style. I popped on the old Sylvania television set and that familiar warm glow filled the room. What wasn't familiar, however, was what appeared onscreen. This was no monster or kitschy tale of private eyes. This wasn't a war movie or a Three Stooges short. This was a newscast...and the most terrifying one I had ever seen.

"It has been established that persons who have recently died have been returning to life and committing acts of murder," said a news reporter. "A widespread investigation of funeral homes, morgues, and hospitals has concluded that the unburied dead have been returning to life and seeking human victims. It's hard for us here to be reporting this to you, but it does seem to be a fact."

My jaw hit the fucking floor like an anvil being dropped from the Road Runner onto the head of the coyote. The reporter went on about having to "get to rescue stations immediately."

HOLY. SHIT. It was the middle of the night. Everyone was sleeping, and only the people like myself who were awake enough to see the news knew what was going on. WHAT LUCK! I had to save my family! We had to find Rob. A million different things started going through my head. This memory remains so vivid to me. I had to move, and do so with the utmost urgency.

I sprang up from the floor and dashed into my parents' bedroom as if the heated licks of a five-alarm fire were hot on my tail. I switched on the light...

"WAKE UP! WAKE UP! THE DEAD ARE COMING! WE GOTTA GO!" I screamed frantically while tugging on my mom's arm. She woke up dazed, and my dad had also begun to stir. I was being a hero. A budding Bruce Campbell if you will. "GET UP! BOTH OF YOU! WE NEED TO GET TO THE RESCUE STATIONS!"

"Stevie, you're having a nightmare," said my mom.

"NO, I AM NOT! IT'S ON THE TV!"

"What the fucking fuck?" asked my visibly annoyed dad. "Go back to fucking bed, will ya? I HAVE WORK IN THE MORNING!"

"NO! WE GOTTA GO! COME, I'LL SHOW YOU! WE HAVE TO GET ROB!"

Finally, my mom sat up, and I dragged her by the arm to the living room with my aggravated dad in tow. At this point, I think he was just more curious than anything else. Well, curious and super pissed off. We made it to the living room, where I pointed to the TV and exclaimed, "LOOK!"

Of course what was on was George A. Romero's 1968 classic *Night of the Living Dead*. "You woke us up because of a movie? A FUCKING MOVIE?!?" snarled my father. I was dumbfounded, and even worse...I was in trouble. BIG TROUBLE. Not only was I up late, not only was I watching TV, but I woke up both the Green and the Brown Gargantua! My words were about to get stuck in my throat and promptly stuffed up my ass.

Punishment was imminent.

My dad took me into my bedroom and grabbed his heavy

leather belt and whipped me on the ass until I could no longer even feel the pain. That was the first time I felt agony. The first time I was actually hit. Mr. Violence was about to become a close friend of mine, and this was our first meeting. He sucked.

After getting his licks in, my dad shut my room light off. As I lay there with my newly tanned ass throbbing, I became aware of something...I was terrified, but I was also 100% safe. How fucking cool is that? The pain subsided after a few moments, and it wasn't long before the monsters had gone back to slumber on Kong Island. Sounds of their sleeping filled my ears, and I did what any other kid in my position should NOT have done...I made my way back into the living room to finish the movie.

It was at that moment that I had what would become my second birth! "Uncle Creepy" had been born. Since then, I've consumed every horror movie I could find. Forever chasing the controlled chaos that horror movies bring. But even then, I knew that *Night of the Living Dead* was different. These weren't monsters inhabiting haunted castles. Every single genre rule that I was familiar with had not only been changed, but they were now "one for the fire."

With *Night of the Living Dead*, George A. Romero and company gave the world a new reason to be scared...and not just of flesh-eating ghouls. This time it was us. Regular people, from regular lives, who lived in regular homes. There were so many "what ifs" running through my head then, and they're still cruising around my brain to this very day.

What if my mom...my friend...my neighbor...the people who loved me...what if they turned? What if their feelings were gone and I was nothing more than a meal? Something to attack and ravage? What if the moment came when I had to decide what to do? Would I have enough courage to put them down? Would that even be showing them mercy? What if, somewhere inside of those shambling bodies, there was a piece of them still alive, and they just couldn't control their bodies? Could I land that perfect headshot if push came to shove? I honestly don't know. Could you?

Night of the Living Dead brought a whole new dimension of reality to the horror genre...one of morals, choices, and true paranoia. Even decades later, this powerful little film has not skipped a beat. This is horror at its finest.

Years later, I got to tell George this story in person. His response? "Hey, man, I am sorry I got your ass kicked!" Anyone who was lucky enough to know him can attest to the fact that his answer was vintage Romero. Typical George.

I'm not gonna soft soap anything...my dad was a bastard. We had a very strained relationship until the day he died. The only thing I ever REALLY learned from him was how I did not want to be...ever. George, through his films, in a lot of ways became the surrogate father I needed. The one who was there for me in my formative years when I had no one. He indirectly taught me the values I needed to become the person that I am, by instilling within me a sense of critical thinking that's been invaluable, to say the least. I could make up my own mind...see things not only in black and white, but in shades of grey...and of course...bloodcurdling color. *Night of the Living Dead* sent me on that journey...and I remain on it. It changed me, along with the rest of the world, and for that I will always be grateful.

Thank you, George. Words cannot describe how much I miss you, brother. I will forever...stay scared.

EVIL DEAD
BY
JOSH MILLICAN

Journalist/Horror Host
Dread Central, Chronic Horror
Facebook: @Joshua.Millican.5
Twitter: @Josh_Millican

I admit it: I used to suffer from a condition known as "knee-jerk remake hate." I immediately called foul on any modern reimagining of a classic horror movie and, as such, I was prepared to loathe Fede Alvarez's *Evil Dead* when it was released in 2013. Instead, I emerged from a midnight screening stunned, shaken, and utterly satisfied. All these years later, it remains one of my absolute favorite horror movies.

Mia (Jane Levy), a drug addict, is determined to kick the habit. To that end, she asks her brother, David (Shiloh Fernandez), his girlfriend, Natalie (Elizabeth Blackmore) and their friends Olivia (Jessica Lucas) and Eric (Lou Taylor Pucci) to accompany her to their family's remote forest cabin to help her through withdrawal. Eric finds a mysterious EBook of the

Dead at the cabin and reads aloud from it, awakening an ancient demon. All hell breaks loose when the malevolent entity possesses Mia.

Alvarez stayed extremely true to the spirit of the original *Evil Dead*, creating an intense visceral experience that was utterly horrifying to behold. But he also included a bold innovation, one that served as both a plot motivator and a brilliant metaphor for a modern social scourge. If the title of this essay didn't already give it away, I'm talking about addiction.

In the original *Evil Dead*, directed by Sam Raimi and starring Bruce Campbell, a group of college students head off to a cabin in the woods for a bit of vacation. In Alvarez's *Evil Dead*, it's a planned detoxification. The film features Mia (played by Jane Levy), a heroin addict who sought out the isolation of the cabin in order to kick the habit.

How many times have we seen horror movies where protagonists ignore blatantly foreboding signs that would send a normal person fleeing in an instant? "So what if half the group is missing and the walls are covered with blood? Let's Party!" Most of the time we cough it up to the stupidity of characters or lack of imagination on the part of writers. That's why Alvarez's use of addiction in *Evil Dead* was a near-genius turn.

If a normal person says, "I smell decomposition; I'm seeing ghosts; I have an overwhelming sense of foreboding," etc., people usually take him or her seriously. If an addict in the throws of withdrawal makes these same claims however, they're easy to dismiss.

Mia's past inability to kick heroin also makes staying at the cabin seem like a rational option, even while additional red flags wave wildly (dead cats in the basement, or a strange book bound in human flesh). Leaving the cabin before she's completely detoxified will be seen as a failure, not just for Mia, but for those who care about her the most. This tough love created a perfect storm for supernatural mayhem.

Fede Alvarez's use of addiction in *Evil Dead* isn't just a brilliant plot motivator, it's an illustration of how perfectly demonic possession works as a metaphor for struggles with extreme dependency. Most often, possession in horror movies is used to explore two key subtexts: mental illness and sexual awakening. The first can be seen in recent offerings like *The Taking of Deborah Logan* and *The Atticus Institute*, while the latter is the crux of just about any possession yarn featuring a teen/young adult woman. While possession remains an impactful springboard for exploring these ideas, *Evil Dead*'s metaphor works, created in the early years of "The Opioid Crisis," however, Alvarez's innovation is both compelling and (dare I say it) important.

Acting like someone unrecognizable to your closest friends and family is a symptom of addiction. Addicts are sometimes described as behaving inhuman, lacking empathy, or prone to violent, even fatal outbursts. Mia's self-mutilations while under Deadite control parallels various forms of physical decay associated with intravenous drug use: track marks, facial sores, deterioration of oral hygiene, etc. Indeed, drug addiction is, by definition, self-destructive.

In addition to being a stellar plot motivator and a creative spin on established subgenre tropes, Alvarez's use of addiction in *Evil Dead* offers a profound way of understanding it. In the film, everyone was so focused on keeping Mia off drugs, they ignored clear signs of danger to themselves. They considered drugs the sole source of Mia's torments, incorrectly assuming that everything will be okay once the chemicals leave her system.

Unfortunately for the characters in the film, Mia's withdrawal was only coincidental; their tunnel-vision caused them to completely miss the real threat to Mia's life (and their own). The message behind the metaphor could be that battling addiction in a vacuum can be ineffective if not downright dangerous.

If you've ever watched shows like *Intervention* or *Dr. Phil*, you've probably heard the term "dual diagnosis". It reflects a change in treating addiction where drug use is regarded as a symptom of a larger problem. Think of it as a curtain that hides the real source of a person's struggle. You can pull down the curtain, but the unknown (or unacknowledged) terror behind it remains.

In other words, had Mia been clean as a bell, the young adults at the cabin still would have faced deadly manifestations of sadistic Sumerian specters.

The possession metaphor for addiction, along with the subtext of multiple underlying issues, was used again and made even more obvious in 2014's *Inner Demons*, directed by Seth Grossman. In that film, a young woman uses heroin to suppress the demons that would otherwise consume her. It addresses a school of thought that only the uninitiated believe: that addicts should simply be able to muster up enough strength to quit.

You can cure an addict from addiction, but unless you have a plan for treating the beast behind the curtain, it's a fruitless battle. Addiction is never the problem in and of itself. It's a shield for even darker demons.

With the semi-recent cancelation of *Ash vs Evil Dead*, fans have been hoping Alvarez may pick up Mia's story in the not-too-distant future. Indeed, Alvarez seemed to gauge interest in the project when he floated the idea past his Twitter followers. The response was tremendously encouraging. Whether or not Mia's story will continue to include elements of addiction remains to be seen.

HALLOWEEN III: SEASON OF THE WITCH

BY

TONY NEWTON

Writer/Director/Producer
VHS Lives: A Schlockumentary, VHS Lives: Undead Format,
Troma's Grindsploitation, Virus of the Dead,
#I'm Zombie, The Zombie Rule Book
Instagram/Twitter: @TonyNewton1

There is only one true face of Halloween.
No, it's not the shape, it's Tom Atkins!

I was 10 years old in 1989, and the holiday of Halloween was all but nonexistent in the UK. No dressing up in wildly gruesome fancy dress costumes, and no trick-or-treating. Halloween was just another day in conservative Britain. In the heavily Catholic country, Halloween held connotations to witchcraft and was perceived as something evil and demonic. But, with the help of Ronald McDonald and his American values, Halloween of 1989 was celebrated.

McDonald's was a new franchise in our seaside town, bringing not only burgers, but delights from The Big Apple such as root beer, hot apple pies, and the best damn milkshakes in the world! McDonald's celebrated all things horror on October the 31st with a Halloween party for kids. At the age of 10, I dressed up as Frankenstein's Monster, bobbed for apples (sharing the saliva of over thirty children), and had a killer time.

Keeping in the Halloween spirit, on the way home, my parents let me rent *Halloween III: Season of the Witch* on VHS from the local video store. With the tape and a free pumpkin from McDonald's in hand, I rushed home and started to carve this strange vegetable whilst watching Halloween on glorious VHS home video!

I had watched horror films before, but *Halloween III* wasn't just a horror film, this was the best damn horror film in the world! I was instantly transfixed, sucked into the world of Halloween, and immersed myself, head on, into the world of horror!

Halloween III is the perfect horror movie. It has everything: synth music, a crazy mask maker tycoon, three of the coolest Halloween masks of all time (the skull, the witch, and the pumpkin), plus a catchy tune that counts down the seven days till Halloween...oh, and a famous moustache!

The premise of *Halloween III* alone is amazing. A small town mask manufacturer splashes the cash for Silver Shamrock TV advertisements, which contain a hidden triggering device designed to kill millions of children at midnight on Halloween. These new masks fast become the must-have Halloween item of 1983.

Unaware of the chip hidden in every mask, the children of the town (and across the globe) watch the midnight special, triggering the devices in the masks to be activated. With the help of an ancient Celtic ritual, using an old ruin from Stonehenge, the masks kill the unsuspecting children. Can Dr. Daniel Challis (Tom Atkins) and Ellie Grimbridge (Stacey Nelkin) save millions of innocent children from the master plan of evil tycoon Conal Cochran (Dan O'Herlihy)?

Mask maker Cochran is a hell of a bad guy, planning to kill millions of children. He's a mix of some kind of messed up form of the Child Catcher from *Chitty Chitty Bang Bang* and your grandfather on crack! In general, children are a taboo subject within film. There aren't many films that show the villain harming or wanting to harm children. There's a scene in John Carpenter's *Assault on Precinct 13* where a young girl gets killed by a gang whilst buying an ice cream. That was unrelenting to watch as a child, let alone an adult. There's something very eerie about Conal Cochran wanting to mass slaughter millions of children.

Thanks to *Halloween III*, I not only have a love for horror and Halloween (my favourite holiday to this day), but I'm obsessed with horror movies. *Halloween III* was a big inspiration for me to write screenplays and produce horror films.

A lot has changed since the late 1980s. Britain now celebrates Halloween, and has heavily done so since the early '90s. Halloween masks, toys, outfits and candy fills the shelves in every supermarket across Britain, and on October the 31st, the streets are filled with trick or treaters. But some things haven't changed. On October the 31st, I still carve a pumpkin and watch *Halloween III* on VHS without fail, now with my wife and son.

Tom Atkins will always be the face of Halloween for me! All hail the moustache!

I'm on a constant quest to evoke the same emotions I felt when watching horror films as a youngster. Seeing *Halloween III* or *Poltergeist* or *The Texas Chain Saw Massacre* or *Cannibal Holocaust* or *Faces of Death* for the first time is a rite of passage for horror fans; as is suffering nightmares that Freddy Krueger can get you in your sleep, where literally nowhere is safe to hide.

These days, horror films that get inside my mind and play on my deepest, darkest fears (like they did when I first watched them as a child) are few and far between, but sometimes I'm knocked sideways when films like *Martyrs*, *Hereditary*, and *Mandy* come along, most certainly keeping horror alive!

Horror films are literally a beast of their own. The subconscious mind can't decipher if what you're experiencing is real or fake, so you will experience real terror while watching one. Your palms will sweat and your heart rate will rise uncontrollably. Horror films are cathartic, and can help you deal with loss, bereavement, and pain on many levels. You can face your deepest, darkest fears head on.

When you're a horror film fan, you're a horror fan for life. No other genre of film can evoke these emotions and give you a roller coaster ride of adrenaline fuelled entertainment like horror can!

HOUSE ON HAUNTED HILL
(1959)
BY
DONALD M. JONES

Director/Editor/Writer/Composer
Murderlust, Project Nightmare, Space-Time In Violet
Twitter: @DnldMarcusJones

How to open a film in the most audacious, over-the-top way possible: start with a completely black, featureless screen. Suddenly a woman's shrill, terrified scream rends the air, followed immediately by the grotesque groaning and hysterical laughing of what apparently is a deep-voiced male ghost. More screaming ensues, accompanied by the obligatory rattling of chains and the creaking of an old door. The screen remains black. A disembodied head, belonging to actor Elisha Cook, Jr. (as character Watson Pritchard), suddenly appears and, while staring straight at us, begins speaking, setting the background for what is about to unfold. A shot of the title's house then appears, over which the disembodied head of Vincent Price as eccentric millionaire Frederick Loren is superimposed. Loren, again speaking directly to us, fills us in further, introducing us to each of the other main characters, all arriving at the house in black hearses in preparation for the haunted house party of all haunted house parties.

This for me, without a doubt, is simply the most effective, spine-chilling opening to a horror film I've ever seen; said film being my favorite horror movie, *House on Haunted Hill* (1959). I was just seven years old when I first viewed it, late one Saturday night on *Chiller*, a local television series featuring horror and science-fiction fare. To this day, nearly sixty years later, I still find it affecting. Audacious.

Then follow several of the best (in my opinion) shock sequences ever, including a marvelously disturbing bit involving a severed head. Over-the-top. Wild. Quite frankly, pretty adult stuff. Were my parents perhaps being a bit irresponsible allowing me, at age seven, to watch this? Well, maybe.

To be sure, plenty of movies scared the living bejesus out of me, including *The Crawling Eye* (aka *The Trollenberg Terror*), *The Thing* (1951), *The Giant Behemoth*, *Invaders from Mars* (1953), *Quatermass 2* (aka *Enemy from Space*), etc. None of them "did the trick" like *House on Haunted Hill*. The surpassingly spooky atmosphere of that malevolent house, the creepy, smooth-talking self assurance of the great Vincent Price, an ensemble of wonderful character actors AND those shock sequences combined to make for a superb haunted house showpiece.

The film's producer/director William Castle, of course, could always be counted on as a showman, particularly when it came to in-theater, live shenanigans. I wish, for example, that I could have seen *House on Haunted Hill* on the big screen and experienced the chills of "Emergo" (where a skeleton on a wire floated above the audience's heads) or watched Castle's *The Tingler* (also starring Vincent Price) where some members of the audience's seats were wired for "shocks".

House on Haunted Hill certainly hard-wired me, often because the most fun I had at the movies afterward was being absolutely and genuinely petrified, something that unfortunately didn't happen often enough. Oh, there were exceptions of course: *The Exorcist*, *Jaws* and *Alien* come to mind. But *House on Haunted Hill* did something to me besides just frighten me – and I think it had to do in part with that great audacious opening.

Fast forward now to July, 1968, when my family and I sat down in the Warner's Theater in Hollywood and watched what was touted as an epic outer space adventure presented in Cinerama. For the next 2 ½ hours, I discovered my life being transformed, and it most certainly began with the spectacularly audacious opening of Stanley Kubrick's *2001: A Space Odyssey* - the monumental alignment of Earth, Moon and Sun, accompanied by colossally majestic music which I had never heard before, but which shook me to the core.

Kubrick once said (to the effect) that the opening image of a motion picture should be the most interesting thing the audience has seen since it first sat down, and that, although he admired beautiful titles with animation and so forth, their use might actually be a distraction, and therefore possibly a detriment to the film's impact. Most of Kubrick's later films have just this sort of impactful start: a simple title followed immediately by an extremely memorable, sometimes jarring opening image. Audacious.

My own experience in making movies, then, could be said to have been profoundly influenced by the powerful emotions wrought by (early on) the terror created by films such as *House on Haunted Hill* and (a bit later) the desire to affect an audience the way Kubrick affected me, particularly when it involved a sense for the audacious. My college buddy James C. Lane (producer, writer) and I (director, editor, occasional writer) had managed to catch the Kubrick virus (acute Stanleyitis) by the early seventies, and in 1975 we made the decision to pursue feature film production full time (or as full time as financial conditions allowed). Our "film school" (other than the countless, silly 8 millimeter flicks I spewed out as a kid) consisted of shooting a little 16 millimeter black and white post-apocalyptic story entitled *Remnants*, which, to the best of our still primitive abilities, had servings of the aforementioned horror (although of a different sort than that found in *House on Haunted Hill*) and audacity (or so we thought). We would go on to make several horror and science-fiction feature films, endeavoring to maintain, among other things, that balance between horror/terror and – hopefully – some measure of audacity.

Start with a completely black, featureless screen...

MY FAVORITE HORROR MOVIE
SCREAM TEAM:

Christian Ackerman has produced over 20 feature films including *Slayer: The Repentless Killogy, Portal, Deadly Reunion, Bethany, Family Vanished,* and two *Stalked By My Doctor* films. As a director, his shorts *Hell's Belles, The Summoners,* and *Watch Your Back* have won over 35 film festival awards.

Felissa Rose came to fame as the star of the iconic *Sleepaway Camp*. Since then, she has produced and/or starred in dozens of films including *Victor Crowley, Stalked By My Doctor: A Sleepwalker's Nightmare, Killer Rose, Hanukkah, Return to Sleepaway Camp, Slayer: The Repentless Killogy,* and *Terrifier 2*.

Chuck Foster is a screenwriter and journalist who co-wrote *The Summoners* and *Watch Your Back*, a featured segment of the *1000 Zombies* anthology. He has contributed to *The Big Takeover, Under the Volcano, The New York Waste, HorrorGarage.com* and, most recently, *Film Threat*. Also a musician, he records and performs in the horror film-influenced synth band Pide Ayuda with his wife Jen Foster (to the occasional roar from his cat Smokey) in NYC.

Designer Josh McKevitt has featured work on several film and TV shows such as *American Horror Story: Cult, Perry Mason, Bliss, Vida* and *The Mindy Project*. One of his many hobbies includes practising prosthetic makeup FX on himself, which led to creating the *My Favorite Horror Movie* cover mascot, Uncle Crusty. He currently resides in Los Angeles with his fiancé Gabrielle and their Welsh "Terror" dog, Lemon.

Printed in Great Britain
by Amazon

55034178R00153